Amos Kidder Fiske

The Myths of Israel, the Ancient Book of Genesis

Amos Kidder Fiske

The Myths of Israel, the Ancient Book of Genesis

ISBN/EAN: 9783744733908

Printed in Europe, USA, Canada, Australia, Japan

Cover: Foto ©ninafisch / pixelio.de

More available books at **www.hansebooks.com**

THE
MYTHS OF ISRAEL

The Ancient Book of Genesis

WITH

ANALYSIS AND EXPLANATION OF ITS COMPOSITION

BY

AMOS KIDDER FISKE

AUTHOR OF "THE JEWISH SCRIPTURES," ETC., ETC.

New York
THE MACMILLAN COMPANY
LONDON: MACMILLAN & CO., Ltd.
1897

All rights reserved

COPYRIGHT, 1897,
By THE MACMILLAN COMPANY.

Norwood Press
J. S. Cushing & Co. — Berwick & Smith
Norwood Mass. U.S.A.

PREFACE

MODERN critical research into the sources and character of the ancient scriptures of the Hebrews leaves no reasonable doubt that the Book of Genesis, which was used as an introduction to the old Jewish law, is a composite production made up largely of myths and fragments of myths embodying the conceptions of the earliest writers of Israel, regarding the relations of that people to their deity. Study of it in this aspect gives it a new interest and significance, while persistence in the old view of its origin and meaning is in danger of sinking it from reverence to derision.

This would be a calamity, because no more remarkable production of ancient genius has been preserved to us, and we may well be grateful for the devoutness, even the superstition, which has kept it through the ages from being buried in the special "sacred writings" of a particular race and a "peculiar" faith. So preserved and made widely familiar, by the gloss and glamour of a sanctity which concealed or perverted its real meaning, it now becomes of extreme interest to the sane student of human development, not only because it contains the early notions of a remarkable race concerning its own origin and destiny, but because within it were planted the first germs of religious conceptions which have grown and expanded through human history and become one of the powerful factors in the gradual elevation of mankind.

The moral tone which pervades the Book of Genesis is not high, and the ethical conceptions of the writers were far from exalted; their ideas of divinity and its working were crude, but, considering the time of the production, the height attained was lofty and luminous amid a vast expanse of moral and religious gloom. The great founders of the Jewish faith laid hold upon the eternal principle of "righteousness" in human conduct and of submission to divine law, so far as it is revealed to human intelligence, and sought to give it a potent sanction in the story of their people.

The story is mythical, the product of imagination and race pride, but in the compact with Abraham and the promise to Jacob was the anchorage of a mighty cord upon which hung the law and the prophets, and to which was appended the gospel of love and peace. Surely it is worthy of study in all the candor of broad enlightenment, and such a study the present writer has endeavored to give it, hoping to lead others who love light rather than darkness to study it in the same spirit.

The text used in this volume is in the main that of the English translation which has been so long familiar, but the two principal versions have been collated with renderings by learned Hebraists, in other languages as well as in English, and liberties have been taken here and there where the real meaning could be made clearer, while some obsolete words and phrases have been superseded, as no special sacredness attaches to the phraseology of King James's time. But an effort has been made not to mar the diction, which has become in a sense consecrated by long familiarity. The old division of chapter and verse, which is largely arbitrary, has been discarded, and a division according to subject has been adopted, without disturbing the traditional arrangement of matter.

For the sake of a readier understanding, the comments and explanations have been interspersed in the form of introductions to the several passages, under new headings. It is the hope of the writer that his labor may contribute to a revival of the study of the oldest of "sacred literature," more intelligent and not less truly devout than that which so long prevailed but which seems to have been dying out because it did not sufficiently appeal to the "common mind" in an age of increasing enlightenment.

A. K. F.

NEW YORK, April, 1897.

CONTENTS

	PAGE
MODERN LIGHT ON ANCIENT SCRIPTURES . . .	3

MATERIAL AND COMPOSITION OF THE BOOK OF GENESIS:
    I. Earliest Writings of the Hebrews . 17
    II. Stories of the Patriarchs 19
    III. Putative Ancestors of Tribes . . 23
    IV. Origin of the Written Tales 27
    V. The First "Sacred History" 31
    VI. The Judean Version 34
    VII. Blending the Two Versions 37
    VIII. Evidences of Late Origin 39

THE TALES AND MYTHS:
    I. The Elohist Account of the Creation . 47
    II. The Jehovist Story of the First Family . . 54
    III. The Antediluvian Generations 67
    IV. The Mixed Account of the Flood . . . 71
    V. Post-diluvian Generations 84
    VI. Abraham takes Possession of the Land . 93
    VII. Abraham as a Warlike Chief . . . 100
    VIII. First Account of the Covenant . . . 106
    IX. First Story of Hagar and Ishmael . . . 110
    X. The Elohist Account of the Covenant . . 114
    XI. Another Version of the Promise of Isaac . . 120
    XII. The Cities of the Plain and the Family of Lot . 123
    XIII. Abraham and Abimelech 133

CONTENTS

		PAGE
XIV.	Second Story of Hagar and her Son	138
XV.	Compact between Abraham and Abimelech	143
XVI.	The Story of offering Isaac	146
XVII.	The Sacred Burial Place	152
XVIII.	The Story of Rebekah	155
XIX.	Varied Progeny of Abraham	164
XX.	Isaac and Abimelech	171
XXI.	The Twin Peoples	177
XXII.	Jacob's Journey to Syria	185
XXIII.	Jacob's Double Marriage	191
XXIV.	The Birth of Jacob's Sons	196
XXV.	Jacob and Laban — Israel and Syria	201
XXVI.	The Division and Treaty	208
XXVII.	Jacob and Esau — Israel and Edom	215
XXVIII.	At Shechem — The Story of Dinah	224
XXIX.	Bethel and after	232
XXX.	Edomite Ethnography	239
XXXI.	Joseph and his Brethren	246
XXXII.	Judah and his Family	255
XXXIII.	Joseph a Slave and in Prison	264
XXXIV.	Joseph's Elevation to Power	272
XXXV.	Joseph's Brothers seek Relief in Egypt	280
XXXVI.	The Second Journey to Egypt	287
XXXVII.	Jacob's Migration	299
XXXVIII.	Settled in Egypt	306
XXXIX.	Strange Results of Famine	312
XL.	Adoption of the Tribes of Joseph	315
XLI.	Poetical Description of the Tribes	322
XLII.	The Burial of Jacob	331
XLIII.	The End of Joseph	336

THE UNKNOWN HOMER OF THE HEBREWS 343

MODERN LIGHT ON ANCIENT SCRIPTURES

MODERN LIGHT ON ANCIENT SCRIPTURES

It is more than two hundred years since Richard Simon, the greatest Oriental scholar of his time, in his "Histoire Critique du Vieux Testament," presented the conclusion to which his study had led him, that the so-called "Books of Moses" were put together by the Scribes of the time of Ezra, making free use of older material. He was assailed by the whole Christian world with such a storm of denunciation, that though he defended his position valiantly, and with a wealth of learning and argument to which his assailants were deaf, he was so overwhelmed with sheer abuse that scholarship was practically silenced on the subject for a century. Though silenced, it did not cease its explorations.

Among its discoveries was a certain difference in what was palpably the oldest material of the Pentateuch in the use of the name of the deity. There was nothing new in the observation that this name was sometimes Elohim and sometimes

Jehovah (Yahweh), but it was found that other marked differences characterized the material in which these terms were severally used in the Book of Genesis and the first chapters of Exodus. The first to set forth these differences in a critical way, and to analyze the material with a view to a clear separation of the component parts, was Dr. Jean Astruc, in the middle of the last century. But such a study of scripture was still so severely discountenanced as to give encouragement rather to the sneering cynicism of Voltaire, than to the conscientious study of devout scholars.

It was not until De Wette began to present the results of his study early in the present century in Germany, that real learning and thought upon this most interesting subject gained sufficient hearing to enter upon the career of conquest which the close of the century is likely to accept as a complete triumph. The two greatest workers in the field for a long time were Ewald at Tübingen and Reuss at Strasburg. Ewald not only had a vast command of Semitic and Oriental lore, but he shrank from no conclusion to which knowledge and reason led him, and he had the courage to state and to defend any position at which he arrived. A great deal still depended upon inference from incomplete data, and upon conjectures supported by uncertain indications, and much of what Ewald put forth was subject to later correction.

The next great advance was made when Abraham Kuenen of Leyden began the publication in 1861 of his history of the origin of the Old Testament books. Other learned scholars were working simultaneously in the same field in Germany and France, notably Nöldeke, Schrader, Graf, Kayser, and Reuss, all tending to the same goal. Kuenen in his later work, the "History of the Religion of Israel," benefited by the results of their labor, and modified some of his earlier conclusions. Professor Edouard Reuss of Strasburg, a Protestant theologian, in his monumental work, "La Bible, Traduction Nouvelle avec Introductions et Commentaires,"— the result of fifty years devoted to study and labor in this field, — candidly accepted the results of research and of honest reasoning and presented them without reserve. Dillman in his laborious commentaries, though conservative in spirit, and cautious in exegesis, accepted the main facts as to the composition of Genesis and other ancient books without dispute. François Lenormant, the French archæologist, author of "The Beginnings of History," versed as no other man of the present generation has been, perhaps, in Chaldean, Syrian, Egyptian, Phœnician, and Hebrew antiquities, and a devout Catholic in his faith, published a translation of "Genesis" in 1883, not only recognizing the composite character of the book, but presenting its component parts distinguished by differences of type.

Finally, the late Ernest Renan, in his "Histoire du Peuple d'Israel," — the crowning work of a lifetime devoted to Semitic learning and to the study of the sources of Judaism and Christianity, — having the advantage of all that had been achieved by his forerunners and contemporaries, and applying to his task the powers of a mind of remarkable lucidity and vigor, adopted the conclusions as to the time and manner of the production of the literature of the Old Testament with the same confidence with which the author of a new history of the people of Ancient Greece would accept the established conclusions of scholars regarding the origin of the early literature of that people. That is practically the attitude on this subject of the present generation of learned theologians and special Biblical scholars on the continent of Europe, of whom the most conspicuous representatives are Julius Wellhausen and Bernhardt Stade.

It was after the results of the research and

critical acumen of Ewald had become familiar, and the riper fruits of the studies of Reuss, Kuenen, and Graf had begun to appear, that Bishop Colenso, in the comparative isolation of South Africa, gave evidence that at least one learned English mind, and that within the pale of the church, was open to the truth on this subject and possessed the candor of its scholarship and the courage of its convictions. But so little prepared was the English mind in general and the sentiment of the English Church in particular, thirty years ago, for an appreciation of such work, that Colenso encountered treatment which was little short of persecution, and which would have embittered the life of a prelate of less patient and serene a spirit; but his work on "The Pentateuch and the Book of Joshua" has conquered its place in the literature of this subject, and is now acknowledged to be "a monument of sound learning, unwearied industry, and of keen critical insight."

The excitement caused by Colenso's writings had scarcely subsided in ecclesiastical circles when Professor William Robertson Smith's contributions to the Encyclopædia Britannica on various Biblical subjects, kindled another, though of much less violence. It was sufficient in the

Presbyterian Church of Scotland to cause his deposition from the professorship of Hebrew at Aberdeen by the General Assembly, but the time had gone by for intolerance toward a scholarship which merely insisted upon telling the truth, and the result for Professor Smith was virtual promotion, for his learning and high character won him a place of honor in the teaching body of one of the great universities of England.

This country has been singularly slow, not merely in accepting the fruits of investigation into the origin of the Jewish Scriptures, but even in acquiring knowledge of them, and sentiment on the subject seems to be backward and unformed, rather than actually hostile, save perhaps in ecclesiastical precincts where traditional views are still tenaciously held. One theologian and scholar within the pale of an orthodox denomination who has candidly and fearlessly taught what he has learned has been rewarded with trials for heresy and efforts to depose him from the Seminary which he has persisted in enlightening, but there have been many evidences that public sympathy even in the Church is largely on his side. Nevertheless, few clergymen venture to tell the truth as many of them know or believe it, because of the unpleasant if not damaging consequences which it is likely to bring upon them.

It had long seemed to the present writer that it would be an acceptable service for some one in this country who was under no restraint of authority and no prescribed obligations, but accountable only to his own intelligence and conscience, to set forth for the common understanding the view of the Old Testament which modern knowledge justifies. He has thought it an advantage that this should be done by one who was not only free from theological prepossessions, but whose working life had not been absorbed in the special study which is liable to narrow the view and impair the sense of proportion. It would be a rare gift if one who had devoted years to close research and a profound study of details should be able to present the broad general results attractively to the unlearned reader. In short, the present writer had the presumption to consider himself particularly qualified to do just what he thought ought to be done and what he has attempted to do in his little work upon "The Jewish Scriptures."

Now he undertakes, perhaps with still greater presumption, to present one example of the ancient Hebrew books, so analyzed and examined as to demonstrate the manner of its production, and, as it seems to him, convincingly to justify the general view which he has taken of the whole collection. Among the conclusions which he takes as established beyond further dispute are these: The first six books of the Old Testament — the Pentateuch and Book of Joshua, or the Hexateuch — which embody the ancient covenants and the Jewish law, were put into their present form after the return from the exile in Babylon, when the Levitical system of the second temple was developed. The code which constitutes the bulk of the Book of Leviticus, but parts of which are reiterated in the last chapters of Exodus and scattered through Numbers and Joshua, was then formulated, and woven somewhat crudely into the old narratives of the early history of the people, which were modified and adapted for the purpose, especially the last sixteen chapters of Exodus and considerable passages in Numbers. The Book of Deuteronomy, which was included in the "Torah," contained the statement of the law, which was put in form in the time of Josiah's reforms, and which the High Priest, Hilkiah, pretended to have found in the temple. The old primitive or "Sacred" history of the people was used as the framework of narrative for the entire system of prescriptions and requirements, and of laws and ordinances for restored Judaism, which it was the special purpose of the priests and Scribes to consecrate. This Sacred History had been compiled in the time of Hezekiah, after the fall of Samaria, and near the end of the eighth century B.C., mainly from two older versions, one of which had been produced in the Northern Kingdom, and the other at Jerusalem, from half a century to a century before. This material constitutes the bulk of the Book of Genesis and the first part of Exodus, and is traceable in fragments through the other books.

In regard to the matters dealt with in the present volume, there is now little dispute among candid scholars, so far as the main facts are concerned. The chief differences of opinion, even among theologians of real learning, relate to what they call the "divine element" working through human means and agencies toward an ultimate result. The present writer has no dispute with those who contend for this "divine element," and who indulge in controversies as to its extent and potency. He acknowledges a divine element in all humanity, a divine energy working in all human history, as it wrought in the development of the physical universe before human history began. He has no doubt of a divine power in the mighty ethical and religious development of the ancient Hebrews, in the beautiful æsthetic development of the ancient Greeks, in the development of the capacity for organization and government in the ancient Romans, and in the combination and inter-working of these factors under the blending influence of Christianity in modern civilization.

Equally divine to his mind is the extension of knowledge through science, research, reasoning, and philosophy in these latter times, correcting the errors of the past, and clearing the eternal verities from the incrustations of ignorance and superstition. It is no less a sacred duty to accept the truth as it is revealed now, than to accept so much of it as may have been contained in what was "said by them of old time." "The eternal years of God" are on the side of truth, and time was never so old and so laden with wisdom as it is to-day. Divine revelation has not been confined to one age or one people, and it never employed human elements and human agencies with more effect than at present.

In analyzing and explaining the Book of Genesis the writer has pursued the same method in detail which he followed in a broad general way in dealing with the whole Old Testament collection. He has studied the work of others with a view to enlightening himself, and then he has studied the production in hand by the light which he has gained. He has not summarized what others have said or discussed their conclusions, and he has felt entirely free to think for himself and present the views which he has reached. The one claim he makes is that of sincerity of purpose and a desire to serve the cause of truth, which is everlasting and always divine.

MATERIAL AND COMPOSITION
OF THE BOOK OF GENESIS

I

EARLIEST WRITINGS OF THE HEBREWS

It is a matter of inference from a variety of indications how early in the history of the ancient Hebrews writing came into use among them. Their language was substantially the same as that of the other Semitic peoples about them, including the Canaanite tribes which they had subjugated, and which were akin to them in origin, and their alphabet was derived from their neighbors on the northwest, the Phœnicians. It must have been late in the period of the "Judges," from eleven to twelve centuries before the Christian era, and two or three centuries, at least, after the invasion of the country of the Canaanites, when the language was reduced to written form, and there is no trace of literary production in that form before the time of David, unless it be found in the statement that the prophet Samuel made a record of the manner of setting up the first kingdom, a statement which is contained in an account compiled long after the event.

The first writings of which we have any actual trace were those which embodied the traditions of the escape from bondage in Egypt and the struggle for the possession of the land occupied at the time the writings were made. These traditions had been preserved by oral repetition, as was common everywhere in primitive times, until they could be gathered up in a more enduring vehicle of transmission.

The "Book of the Wars of Jehovah" and the "Book of Jasher"—whether these were independent productions or parts of one collection cannot be clearly determined from the scanty references—were the first receptacle of the legends connected with the invasion and conquest of Canaan, and the conflicts which preceded the establishment of the Kingdom. The lament of David over the death of Saul and Jonathan is said by the compiler of the Book of Samuel to be written in the "Book of Jasher," which indicates, at least, that the collection had not been closed when David became the King of Judah. This collection of the traditions of Israel's heroic age appears to have furnished much of the material or many of the suggestions for the narratives of the Books of Judges and Samuel, and for some of the episodes of the escape from Egypt and the conquest of Canaan, including those of the late and artificial account of Joshua's exploits.

II

STORIES OF THE PATRIARCHS

IT is pretty clear that it was after the division of the Kingdom and the establishment of Jeroboam as the first ruler of the Northern realm that the ethnic myths, known as the "Stories of the Patriarchs," first appeared. It has been common, even for those who admit that their original production could not have been earlier than that time, to assume that they were based upon traditions of the Nomadic days before the migration into Egypt, preserved from generation to generation by oral transmission, but that is extremely doubtful. Considering the variety of ethnic and mythic meanings still traceable in these tales and their many points of contact with the relations, purposes, and ideas of the time and place of their production, it is more likely that they were the imaginative offspring of the genius of that time and place.

The aspects of Nomadic life were still familiar in the neighboring plains on the east, and the Nomadic instinct of the Hebrews was always yearning for its freedom and simplicity. It inspired the ideals which determined their aspirations and rendered them weak as an organized nationality. And yet, there is no clear evidence that they carried memories or definite traditions of their own Nomadic days through the dark bondage in Egypt and the long struggle from the deliverance to the conquest. The impress of the infant days of their race was indelible; the tendency then begotten never died, and there were, no doubt, cherished associations of name and place that survived through ages of trial, but the actual persons and deeds of their ancestry were utterly forgotten.

When their first writers began to supply this lack by their own creations, the two kingdoms of Judah and Ephraim, the latter monopolizing the ancient name of Israel, were at the height of the antipathy engendered by the division of the first kingdom, and were engaged in their earliest rivalry as separate nations, with Ephraim the stronger and more confident. Being the immediate neighbor of Phœnicia and having as its ruler a man of uncommon ability and energy, who had enjoyed the advantage of a long sojourn in Egypt under the favor of the monarch of that country, Ephraim entered upon a period of intellectual and literary activity of which Judah, under the feeble and reactionary reign of Rehoboam, the son of Solomon, showed no sign. It was at this time, in the Kingdom of the North, that the patriarchal stories first appeared. They are usually spoken of as a collection, but they seem to have formed a series with no clear sequence or coherency, and they underwent variations which in time produced different versions.

If we recall the situation of the time we shall find the Kingdom of Israel (Ephraim) in the first flush of its pride and power, with a sense of superiority over Judah, mingled with a degree of fraternal enmity; with a kindly feeling toward Egypt, and friendly relations with Syria, and with a scorn for the subjugated tribes of Canaan. Associated with Ephraim was the closely related tribe of Manasseh and the Northern provinces, which had names that were rather territorial than tribal, and there was a disposition to detach from Judah, the warlike community of Benjamin, which lay on the division line, and which had furnished the first king of all Israel, whose dynasty had been cut short by David.

There were rooted enmities for the Edomites and Moabites, which were common to all the tribes, and had been inherited from the time of the long struggle through the deserts on the way to the conquest of the land of the Canaanites, for the hostile spirit of those peoples had added to the length and the hardships of the struggle. There had been many a conflict with the Ammonites who were akin to Moab, and with the predatory Amalekites of the South, and these also were rated as hereditary enemies.

The dominant sentiment of Israel was pride of race and a sense of superiority, though the ancient relationship of the Semitic peoples of the whole region from the "Great River" to the sea, and to the "River of Egypt," including the Ishmaelites and Midianites of the Arabian desert, was acknowledged, save that the subjugated and despised Canaanites were cut off from that noble stock. The victims of conquest and of the sentiment engendered by it, were relegated to an inferior origin, and ejected from the family in which they were born. Knowledge of the great eastern Empire of the Tigris and Euphrates was imperfect and somewhat vague, and all beyond to the east and north, was mystery. There was a tradition that the Hebrews — a name that signified "from beyond" — had originally migrated from the northern plains of Mesopotamia (Paddan-aram).

III

PUTATIVE ANCESTORS OF TRIBES

ABRAM, or Abraham, was a revered name among all the Semitic peoples, and the Syrians, Arabians, and Phœnicians, as well as the Hebrews, had their separate lines of tradition connecting with it. It even figured in the fabulous history of the Chaldæans. When the Israelites began to produce their ethnic myths, explaining and glorifying their origin, their superiority, and their special claim to the land of which they had taken possession, and to exalt their God above all other deities, they appropriated as peculiarly their own the fatherhood of Abraham and relegated to an inferior position all the other reputed progeny of Terah, who had come from the mysterious land of "Ur of the Chaldees."

The Ishmaelites and Midianites were allowed to be of a direct descent from Abraham, but in an inferior sense. A close relation was permitted to the Edomites, but they were humiliated to a secondary place. The Syrians were set off on a collateral branch as descendants of Abraham's brother Nahor, while the hated Moabites and Ammonites were placed on another line with the stamp of death and incest on their origin. The Israelites alone were of the pure strain of Abram, the "high father," who became Abraham, the "father of many," the favored offspring of Sarai ("the princess"), doubly sanctified by divine promise and by birth in her old age, after a long life of barrenness.

There were traditions of an ancient branch of the Hebrew family on the Philistine border in the south, about the old fane of Beersheba, or the Seven wells. This had died out, and the traditions were dim, but the name of Isaac ("laughter") remained, and the Beersheba region, though in the south, was associated much more closely with Ephraim than with Judah. The general name for the Hebrew tribes in their union had been Israel from a time that is immemorial now, if it was not then. Many writers assume that it antedated the Egyptian bondage. According to the generally accepted etymology it meant "warrior of God." The Hebrews were not essentially a warlike people, and they could hardly have given themselves that title in the Nomadic days. It more probably sprang out of the one era in their history, when they were nerved to desperate battle for the possession of a country which they claimed by inheritance and divine promise, and when their deity became a "God of battles." It is more likely that Israel was adopted as a general title by a people engaged in a war of conquest, than by one roaming about with flocks and herds, or dwelling in servitude in a foreign land.

Jacob was a poetical designation for the same people, and used only in rhetorical language. It was derived from a word meaning "heel," and was applied to one who supplanted or superseded another. There is no indication of its use before the tribes were established as a nation, and its adoption probably had reference rather to the crushing or supplanting of the Canaanites than to any relation with the comparatively remote Edomites. The dominant tribes of the Northern Kingdom were poetically designated as Joseph, the double derivation of which may have a special significance. It is explained as meaning both taking from and adding to. It may imply an original joining to the other tribes, or a separation from them in their later history, and it was used with apparent reference to both senses. There were traditions of a tribe or branch of the Hebrew people which had settled in the south under the name of Simeon, but which had faded out, and of two that had remained to the east of the Jordan after the conquest, designated as Reuben and Gad, which had also lost their distinct identity. There was a class of persons scattered over the country, and wandering from place to place, associated chiefly with the oracles and shrines of worship, and known as sons of Levi, that being a general term borrowed from Egypt for those who served at altars.

Most tribal and territorial names in those days had some meaning derived from characteristics of the people, or of the country which they occupied, or from some incident in their history, though derivations were frequently assumed from the superficial resemblance of proper names to words in common use, with which they had really no etymological relation. Both tribal and territorial names were often personified, and taking possession of a land was sometimes represented as the marriage of a man bearing the name of the tribe with a woman bearing the name of the country, while clans and provinces figured as their children.

IV

ORIGIN OF THE WRITTEN TALES

JEROBOAM had established his seat of power at Shechem, which had been the scene of the turbulent effort of Abimelech, the son of Gideon, to make himself king. Near by was Shiloh, where it was said that the Ark of the Covenant had long "rested," and where the priests had received their offerings and made their sacrifices in the old days, but the temple at Jerusalem had become a centre of worship, and Jeroboam deemed it expedient to establish his principal altar farther away. He placed it on the height at Bethel, which, under the name of Luz, had been a sacred place of the Canaanites, and sought to make it attractive by symbols of worship similar to those of Egypt.

The material for the stories of the patriarchs existed in the names of places, of nations, tribes, and clans, in the various characteristics of these and their relations with each other, and in traditions of events and circumstances to many of which we have found no tangible clue. Their chief motive was to exalt Israel and degrade its enemies, to trace its possession of the country to divine promise and divine aid, and to explain, in a manner that glorified rather than degraded it, the falling into Egyptian slavery. Incidentally, in their development they were made to impress lessons and warnings relating to the ethics and religion of the time of their production.

In outline, the ancestral story was that the father of Abraham had wandered from the remote and mysterious land of "Ur of the Chaldees" in the East and settled in Aram of the rivers (Paddan-aram). There the brother of Abraham, Nahor (that being the name of a place), had become the ancestor of Syria, and another brother, Haran (also the name of a place), had died. With his wife Sarah (princess) and his orphaned nephew (Lot), Abraham went into the land of Canaan, where he was to become the progenitor of many peoples, and the specially sanctified ancestor of the Israelites, and where the nephew was to become the forefather of the Moabites and Ammonites on the other side of the lower Jordan and in the region beyond the Dead Sea.

Abraham took possession of the land by passing through it and setting up altars at Shechem and Bethel and at Beersheba, and went on into

Egypt, where the divine care over his life was exhibited. The Judean version of the story associated him especially with Hebron, the first scene of David's royalty, where his possession of the land was consecrated by purchasing a permanent burial place. The name of "Isaac," associated with the Beersheba region, was given to the son of Abraham's old age, and for him a wife of the blood of his father's family was obtained, and from that union came Jacob, who married in Syria and begat the heads of all the tribes. Joseph was a favorite son and had been carried captive to Egypt, as the result of the envy and spite of his brothers, there to be exalted to power and to become the saviour of the family.

In filling in this outline with a variety of details the first writers took occasion to explain in the forms of personal story not only the separation of Lot from Abraham and the opprobrious origin of Moab and Ammon, but the elimination from the heritage of the chosen people of Ishmael and Edom and the birth of Midian and the kindred people of the desert. They undertook to account for the division of possessions with Syria in the northeast and with the Philistines of the southwest, and to explain the origin of the "Covenants," which were assumed to be the peculiar bond between the people of Israel and their God, and the basis of their worship and their sacred law. How much of this kind of literature may originally have existed in oral form, and how much may have been altogether lost in the process of preservation in writing, we have no means of knowing, but we can plainly see that what was preserved became wrought into a marvellous patchwork. The seams are still visible and the colors do not entirely harmonize, but the effect produced has been deeper and more lasting than that of any other creation of human genius in its pristine vigor.

V

THE FIRST "SACRED HISTORY"

THE most striking single embodiment of the early Hebrew genius appeared in the writer who produced the first "sacred history" of the "peculiar people." He was of the Northern Kingdom of Israel, and his time, as nearly as it can be determined, was that of the reign of Jehu, at Samaria, in the middle of the ninth century B.C., when the spirit of "prophecy" was first awakened, and a fierce conflict was waged against the tendency to lapse into the ways and the worship of Phœnicia, to which a strong impulse had been given in the days of Ahab, when the Tyrian queen Jezebel exercised so much influence. This writer, whose name and identity are lost in the mists of antiquity, was contemporary with the mysterious personality behind the legendary names of Elijah and Elisha, and it is a fascinating conjecture that he may have been identical with that personality.

His main purpose was to lay down rules of

conduct and requirements of worship for the people of Israel, and to give these the most solemn and impressive sanction. This sanction was to be derived from the covenants of Jehovah with the ancestors of the people and his promises to their posterity, and to be confirmed by the deliverance from Egyptian bondage and the possession of the land of Canaan in fulfilment of promise. The worship of Jehovah was to be exalted and sanctified and made a matter of such terrible obligation as to be a bulwark against the enticements of Baal and Astarte ("Ashtoreth").

This writer had some familiarity with the fables of Babylon and Nineveh, and with the mythology of Phœnicia, and he began his story with the creation of the world and the origin of the human race, deriving his material from those foreign sources, but giving it the impress of his own potent genius. He made large use of the legends already existing in written form, of Abraham, Isaac, and Jacob, and the sons of Jacob, developing and varying them to suit his purpose, and he used, in a continuance of his history after the period of Egyptian bondage, material from the "wars of Jehovah," and traditions of Moses, Miriam, and Aaron, and the trials of the long journey through the wilderness, blending these elements into a narrative which had a certain epic grandeur.

So much as has been preserved of the production of this Northern writer forms what is called the Jehovist material in the Hexateuch, and from it a considerable part of the Book of Genesis was derived. The term Jehovist (or "Yahwist") is employed because the writer used the name Jehovah, or Yahweh, for the deity, that being the name in common use at the time, which was assumed to have been first adopted in the wilderness, when Moses had just rescued the people from their servitude within the borders of Egypt and was rallying them to the tremendous effort of making their way to the possession of the promised land.

VI

THE JUDEAN VERSION

It was but a few years after the time of the Jehovist that the writer known as the Elohist put forth at Jerusalem the Judean version of the "Sacred History." Such of his work as has been preserved is known as the Elohist material, or from the "Elohist document," because he used the word "Elohim" for the deity down to the point in the narrative at which the appellation of Jehovah was said to have been revealed to Moses. There had been as yet no such religious ferment in Judah as had been going on in the Northern Kingdom, and the prophetic spirit had not begun that vigorous development which culminated in Isaiah. Writing had been mainly devoted to genealogies and rude annals, and the Elohist was rather of the priests than the prophets.

He was familiar with the common traditions of the Hebrew people, and with some of the stories which had sprung up around the names of the tribes, and had some knowledge of the fabulous lore of Babylon and Assyria. He had much less familiarity than the Northern writer with the learning of Egypt, and possessed little of the creative faculty of the Jehovist, his form of statements being more prosaic. He began with an account of the creation, derived from the Chaldean cosmogony, but it had rather the quality of an infantile science than of a poetic mythology. The Chaldean division of time into periods of seven days, fourths of the lunar month, and the Assyrian practice of devoting the seventh day to rest and worship had come into vogue, and this writer sought to give it a special sanctity in his description of the creation. He it was who embodied the "decalogue" in his narrative, and in it consecrated the Sabbath as the day on which the Lord rested after creating "heaven and earth and sea and all that in them is." When this little code in a somewhat different form was incorporated in the law in Jeremiah's day, the Sabbath was hallowed in remembrance of the deliverance from Egyptian bondage.

Both the Jehovist and the Elohist adopted with some variation the Babylonian story of the destruction of mankind by a universal flood, and the latter endeavored to fill the intervals between the creation and the flood, and between the flood and the migration of Abraham, with regular genealogies, or "generations," of the families of the earth before Israel was born, using for the purpose the geographical names within his knowledge.

In fact, the Elohist's work was largely genealogical and ethnographical, and he made scanty use of the patriarchal stories. The Northern versions of them were probably unknown to him, and he did not have the genius for developing such tales which the writer of Ephraim possessed. He was more intent upon tracing religious customs to an ancient origin, and it was he who sanctified circumcision as the seal of the covenant with Abraham. The practice was neither religious nor Israelite in its origin, but the Israelites had brought it into the land of Canaan, and there insisted upon its sacredness as a badge of their separation from all other peoples, and made it the most rigidly observed rite of their peculiar faith.

VII

BLENDING THE TWO VERSIONS

AFTER the fate of Samaria in 721 B.C., such of the literary treasures of the Kingdom of Israel as were fortunately preserved were added to those of Judah, which had been accumulating at Jerusalem, and a few years later, during the active and productive period of the reign of Hezekiah, some writer, probably of the temple scribes, undertook to combine into one, the two versions of the sacred history. He appears to have had other material at his command, and did not refrain altogether from injecting statements of his own. He was by no means a skilful or painstaking compiler, and he preferred copying and piecing together his material to recomposing it into a new and harmonious narrative, and even when he attempted to modify a statement of his predecessors, he often did it so clumsily as to leave evidence of inconsistency.

This writer had the Judean point of view, and was accustomed to the use of Jehovah (or Yahweh) as the name of the Deity; but the shorter Elohist document was the basis of his compilation, so far as it went, and where he pieced passages of the other into it he made no changes in the divine name. Where he had two versions of the same proceeding, he usually adopted one in preference to the other, but sometimes he undertook to combine them in order to save different details, and sometimes where they varied rather widely he used both, as if they referred to different proceedings. Occasionally he introduced fragments of material quite independent of his two main documents, and formed connecting links of narrative of his own.

That so much of the Northern production was preserved, notwithstanding its exaltation of Ephraim and disparagement of Judah, was due in part to the perfunctory manner of the compiler, and in part, no doubt, to the softening of old antipathies after the calamities of Israel and the destruction of Samaria, and to the hope that was now cherished of the ultimate reunion of the tribes under one king of the house of David.

VIII

EVIDENCES OF LATE ORIGIN

THERE is little evidence that, during the interval between the compilation of this sacred history and the taking of Jerusalem by the Babylonians, its contents had become familiar even to the prophets and writers of the period. One of the strongest evidences that the oldest material in the narrative was later than the time of Solomon, and was unfamiliar until after the captivity, is to be found in the absence of all allusion to what it embodies in the other writings of the time of the kingdoms. In the books of Judges, Samuel, and Kings there is no sign of a knowledge of the venerable ancestors of the race, or even of Moses and his "law," save for the latter in passages of the later annals distinctly traceable to redaction after the exile.

Not only is there no sign of such knowledge, but the whole tone and spirit of the narratives and the character of their contents are inconsistent with its existence. In the later literature we meet with the names Israel and Jacob and

Joseph, as well as Ephraim and Judah, in their general national application, but with no reference to such personalities as Abraham, Isaac, and Jacob, and the sons of Jacob.

The prayer put in the mouth of Solomon at the dedication of the temple by the late compiler of the annals of his reign, is anachronistic and out of keeping with the character, but while it contains repeated appeals to the "God of Israel," there is no recognition of the God of Abraham, Isaac, and Jacob. In the strange passage which represents the prophet Elijah as praying to Jehovah in competition with the prophets of Baal, he invokes the "God of Abraham, of Isaac, and of Israel," but elsewhere in the annals, from the conquest to the doom of the kingdom, these venerable names do not appear, and the appearance of this phrase in the story of Elijah reminds us of the coincidence of time and similarity of character in the production of the Jehovist document and the legend of the prophet of Carmel.

The phrases, "the posterity (or seed) of Abraham, Isaac, and Jacob" and "the covenant with Abraham, Isaac, and Jacob," are common in the Book of Deuteronomy, and the former appears once in the writings of Jeremiah, who was almost certainly associated with the production of that book, at a time when the literature of the temple already contained the "sacred history" as it had been compiled in the days of Hezekiah. Isaiah used the names Abraham and Jacob only in the ethnic sense, and the former occurs only once in the writings of the first, or real, Isaiah. He shows no knowledge of the patriarchs of Israel. Micah uses the name of Abraham once, but in the strictly ethnic sense. Hosea alone of the prophets shows some evidence of familiarity with the legend of Jacob, but he was of the Northern Kingdom, and near the time of the legend's origin. Amos, who dwelt near the Beersheba region, where the Isaac tradition prevailed, is the only one to use that name even in its ethnic sense before the captivity, save in the phrase of Jeremiah already referred to.

The conclusion is irresistible that nothing was known, in the land of Israel, of the patriarchs, or of the stories in which their names figure, until after the period which is now assigned by learned critics for the production of those stories, and that knowledge of the Sacred History in which they were incorporated was confined to a small class until after the captivity, when the books of the law were promulgated. There is no trace of an oral tradition of the personalities or the families of the so-called ancestors of the Israelites during the long period anterior to the division of the kingdom, and the development of written literature, and if it had existed it could hardly have escaped some passing allusion. The use of personal names to designate tribes or bands, and the putting of tribal history into the form of personal story, were common everywhere in primitive times, especially among Oriental peoples. The Israelites usually spoke of the people of a land as the children of the land, and the Hittites, a much older people than themselves, were called the children of Heth, Heth being assumed to be the name of an ancient personage. There is a curious illustration of the practice of the first writers in personifying tribes in their ordinary language, at the beginning of the Book of Judges, where, several generations after the era assigned to Jacob's family, "Judah said unto Simeon his brother, 'come up with me into my lot, that we may fight against the Canaanites, and I likewise will go with thee into thy lot.' So Simeon went with him."

Apparently the Book of Genesis underwent little change after the compilation in the time of Hezekiah. It must have been among the literary treasures of the temple, which were carried from Jerusalem to Babylon and preserved through the captivity, and after the return it was made the first section of the Torah, as containing the ancient covenants upon which the early writers had based the law in its rudimentary form. It needed little change to adapt it to the purpose. It was designated only by its opening words, and the present title was first attached to it in the Greek version of the Pentateuch known as the Septuagint. The circumstances and method of its production make it the most compact and remarkable repository of the first conceptions of primitive genius that has been preserved in human history. The seal of sacredness put upon it by the doctors of Judaism deterred for ages all attempt at an analysis of its composition, but the daring of modern scholarship has at last resolved it into its elements.

THE TALES AND MYTHS

I

THE ELOHIST ACCOUNT OF THE CREATION

THE compiler, as we shall call the writer who in the time of Hezekiah wrought the "Sacred History" out of materials furnished by his predecessors, began with the Elohist's account of the creation, which occupies the first chapter and the first three verses of the second chapter of Genesis, as it came to be divided long afterwards. The author of this knew something of the Chaldean fable on the subject. It is not necessary to assume that this knowledge came through long tradition from the time when the Semitic tribes wandered as Nomads on the borders of Mesopotamia, for there was not an absolute lack of communication with that land in the writer's own day.

The system of six days for labor and the seventh for rest was of Chaldean origin, had long been in use in Assyria, and was already established in Judah. The account of the creation was made to give a special sanction to the observance of the Sabbath, which had come to be a requirement of the religion of the temple. Otherwise, there is an infantile simplicity in the quasi science of the description, in marked contrast with the mystical tendency of the Jehovist writer.

The infantile simplicity of the writer's conception of the physical universe is manifest in every phase of the six days' work of creation. He conceives first of the earth as a mass of water weltering in darkness, and of the appearance of light and the alternation of day and night in advance of the existence of the luminaries that were to rule the day and night and determine the seasons. His notion of the firmament was that of a solid barrier holding a mass of water above the earth, forming the reservoir of rain and storms. The same general idea appears in the Book of Job and some of the older Psalms, writings of substantially the same age as this.

In order to keep to the six days for labor two processes are crowded into the third day. The dry land is made to appear by the simple process of gathering the waters that were left below the firmament into one place, which hardly conforms to any real physical geography, and then vegetation is brought forth in advance of the creation of the sun with its vivifying influences. The classification into grass assumed to be seedless, plants that bear seed, and fruit trees, is of the most primitive order. The sun, moon, and stars are created after there have been three alternations of night and day, and after the earth has been clothed with vegetation.

A day is devoted to the production of the denizens of the water and the air, and on the sixth day the animals that occupy the earth are brought into being and roughly classified as cattle, reptiles, and beasts. Then comes the crowning work of man's creation in the image of God. This was strictly according to the anthropomorphic conception of the ancient Hebrews. Other divinities might have the likeness of beasts, but their deity had the semblance and qualities of an exalted man. The exaltation was so sublimated as to make it the height of presumption to provoke comparison by material representations of God. Hence the aversion not only to idols, but to all portrayals of the human form. The account closes with assigning the grass or "green herb" to the animals for sustenance, and the cereal plants and fruit of trees to man. In the mind of this writer there was no eating of flesh in the infant days of the world.

It is needless to say that the physical science of this account is the fancy of a primitive age, and bears no relation to the actual origin of things. But the real significance of the production lies in its embodiment of an exalted conception of the almightiness of God, who wrought all things out of nothing by the mere exercise of his will, and in the acceptance of the work of God as altogether good. The sublimity of this conception of monotheism so glorifies the account of creative processes that we lose sight of the crude absurdities of the details.

[I-II 4]

IN the beginning God [Elohim] created the heaven and the earth. The earth was waste and void; and darkness brooded upon the face of the deep; and the spirit of God moved upon the face of the waters. And God said, Let there be light: and there was light. And God saw the light, that it was good; and God divided the light from the darkness.˙ And God called the light Day, and the darkness he called Night. And there was an evening and a morning, one day.

And God said, Let there be a firmament in the midst of the waters, and let it divide the waters from the waters. And God made the firmament, and divided the waters which were under the firmament from the waters which were above the firmament: and it was so. And God called the firmament Heaven. And there was an evening and a morning, a second day.

And God said, Let the waters under the heaven be gathered together unto one place, that the dry land may appear: and it was so. And God called the dry land Earth; and the gathering together of the waters called he Seas: and God saw that it was good. And God said, Let the earth put forth grass, herb yielding seed, *and* fruit tree bearing fruit after its kind, wherein is the seed thereof, upon the earth: and it was so. And the earth brought forth grass, herb yielding seed after its kind, and tree bearing fruit, wherein is the seed thereof, after its kind; and God saw that it was good. And there was an evening and a morning, a third day.

And God said, Let there be lights in the firmament of the heaven to divide the day from the night; and let them be for signs, and for seasons, and for days and years; and let them be for lights in the firmament of the heaven to give light upon the earth: and it was so. And God made the two great lights; the greater light to rule the day, and the lesser light to rule the night; he made the stars also. And God set them in the firmament of the heaven to give light upon the earth, and to rule over the day and over the night, and to divide the light from the darkness; and God saw that it was good. And there was an evening and a morning, a fourth day.

And God said, Let the waters bring forth abundantly the moving creature that hath life, and let fowl fly above the earth in the open firmament of heaven. And God created the great sea-monsters, and every living creature that moveth, which the waters brought forth abundantly, after their kinds, and every winged fowl after its kind; and God saw that it was good. And God blessed them, saying, Be fruitful, and multiply, and fill the waters in the seas, and let fowl multiply in the earth. And there was an evening and a morning, a fifth day.

And God said, Let the earth bring forth the living creature after its kind, cattle, and creeping thing, and beast of the earth after its kind; and it was so. And God made the beast of the earth after its kind, and the cattle after their kind, and every thing that creepeth upon the ground after its kind; and God saw that it was good. And God said, Let us make man in our image, after our likeness; and let them have dominion over the fish of the sea, and over the fowl of the air, and over the cattle, and over all the earth, and over every creeping thing that creepeth upon the earth. And God created man in his own image, in the image of God created he him; male and female created he them. And God blessed them; and God said unto them, Be fruitful, and multiply, and replenish the earth, and subdue it; and have dominion over the fish of the sea, and over the fowl of the air, and over every living thing that moveth upon the earth.

And God said, Behold, I have given you every herb yielding seed, which is upon the face of all the earth, and every tree, in which is the fruit of a tree yielding seed; to you it shall be for food; and to every beast of the earth, and to every fowl of the air, and to every thing that creepeth upon the earth, wherein there is life, I have given every green herb for food: and it was so. And God saw every thing that he had made, and, behold, it was very good. And there was an evening and a morning, the sixth day.

And the heaven and the earth were finished, and all the host of them. And on the seventh day God finished his work which he had made; and he rested on the seventh day from all his work which he had made. And God blessed the seventh day, and hallowed it, because that in it he rested from all his work which God had created and made.

[These are the generations of the heaven and of the earth when they were created.]

II

THE JEHOVIST STORY OF THE FIRST FAMILY

If the Jehovist gave any account of the creation of the earth, it was omitted by the compiler, who apparently interpolated the statement "these are the generations of the heaven and of the earth," with reference to what precedes and for the purpose of connecting the two fragments. He left traces of a radical difference of view as to the origin of things, for where the Elohist represents the land as emerging from a waste of waters, the Jehovist assumes an arid waste of land in need of rain to make it fruitful. The latter's conceptions were more mythological in quality and he was evidently more familiar with Babylonian and Phœnician fable, which he used in a fragmentary way and transmuted with the touch of an original genius.

The peculiarly anthropomorphic character of his conception of the deity is evident throughout. Instead of the mysterious Elohim bringing all things into being by the fiat of his will, we have the Yahweh who forms man out of the dust of the ground and breathes into him the spirit of life. He plants a garden and places the man in it to dress and keep it. Out of the ground he makes the trees to grow for the delight of the eye and to furnish food, and out of the ground he forms the birds and beasts, after he has made man from the dust, and brings them to man to receive their names. Woman he creates to be man's helpmeet by taking of his substance and moulding it ("building" in the original) into her form. It is a story-book account of making living things.

In it there are suggestions of primitive derivation. The notion that man came from the dust and returned to the dust was prevalent in the Hebrew philosophy, and an etymological relation was assumed between *adam*, the general term for man, and *adamah*, earth. Hence the making of man from the dust of the ground. Such a relation did exist between *is*, man, in the special sense of "vir" as distinguished from "homo," and *issah*, woman. Hence the making of woman from the substance of man, in conformity with the saying already proverbial, bone of his bone and flesh of his flesh. The saying that a man shall leave his father and mother and cleave unto his wife can seem appropriate in a being who has had no father and mother and beholds a woman for the first time, only as a mythical embodiment of general truths concerning human society.

The word "Eden" meant rather a place or condition of delight than a special location, and the matter-of-fact description with reference to the rivers of the primitive world (in brackets below) is an interpolation of the compiler. The Hiddekel was the Tigris, but the rivers Pishon and Gihon, which were made to compass the regions of the East and South, correspond to no actual streams. In the writer's imperfect geography the names may have stood for remote rivers of which he had only a vague notion.

The mythic significance of the story of the first human couple was lost for ages through a perversion of its meaning to serve the ends of a dogma wrought in perfect good faith by the early teachers of Christianity. It symbolizes the infancy of the race as a state of childhood, in the innocence and delight of "Eden," unconscious of either good or evil, knowing neither wisdom nor folly, caring not for its nakedness. But it cannot remain in its "clouds of glory." The unhappy time comes for the stirring of the insidious desire for knowledge of good and evil and the impulse to liberty of action. That suggestion of developing human nature is symbolized in the serpent popularly credited with subtlety and wisdom among animals by the ancients.

The stirring and yearning of that time of change comes sooner in woman than in man, and she is apt to afford the incitement and stimulus to it in him; and, when it comes, the state of guileless innocence is ended. With the knowledge of good and evil comes the consciousness of shame in nakedness. On that day, too, comes death,— not literally, but in apprehension and sense of certainty, and man is turned out of his garden of delight to face the toil of life and woman to meet the pain and sorrow of motherhood.

But why was the eating of the fruit forbidden? Is there not in this an expression of sadness that man should persist in knowing and doing for himself, and so incur the penalties of achievement, and of a divine solicitude that he might remain innocent and happy and forever a child? Once tasting of knowledge and coming to the choice of good and evil, he is debarred from the tree that would furnish the antidote to the bitter penalty. The cherubim and a flaming sword guard the domain of innocent childhood which he has left.

In this symbolizing of a universal truth in human nature and human life there is no suggestion of individual sin or even of general sin. There is no suggestion of a spirit of evil in the serpent, but his supposed subtlety as a beast is used to figure the first awakening of the desire for knowledge of good and evil; and the antipathy between him and man is attributed to a primal curse. When the strangely man-like God walks in the garden the shrinking from his presence is not from a sense of guilt, but of nakedness. The sad turn has come in human life and character when nudity implies shame. "Who told thee that thou wast naked?"

The doctrine of original sin, of the fall from a state of perfection, and the loss of an immortal condition, was never drawn from this myth by the Jews, because it was not embodied in it by their genius. It was not in keeping with their ideas, and the story was really an allegory of the growth and not the fall of man,—an expression of human development and not of relapse. The later doctrine was laboriously wrought to serve as the basis of another,—that of the redemption of a fallen race, whose fall was thus accounted for.

The Cain and Abel myth is separate from that of Adam and Eve, and had in part the purpose of illustrating the tendency of the human race to violence and bloodshed. The innocent offspring of the first couple was destroyed and the depraved and vengeful was sent forth into the land of wandering (Nod) to people the world alone. There is a curious naïveté in the assumption that it already contained people from whom he needed protection and among whom he must have found the wife that bore Enoch, which was the name of a city still known in the time of the writer. Incidently this story is used to enforce the idea that the "firstlings of the flock and the fat thereof," rather than the "fruit of the ground," were the proper and accepted "offering unto the Lord"; and it contains the undeveloped germ of the primitive division of human occupations into tilling the soil and caring for flocks, and gives a sort of sanctity to the latter as having been that of the forefathers of Israel.

The obscure traces of myth in the brief passage relating to Cain's descendants are from a Phœnician source, and bear upon the supposed origin of pastoral people and of artificers of tools and weapons, and of musical instruments, the sole products of primitive mechanical skill. Tubal-Cain and Naamah are believed to have had a remote relationship to Vulcan and Venus, but the material, of which the words of Lamech to his wives appear to be an ancient rhythmical fragment, was used so sparingly as to leave the whole passage in obscurity. The statement as to the birth of Seth does not belong to the Jehovist document, but was drawn by the compiler from the Elohist to supply the place of Abel, and to connect this with the passage which follows in the compilation. The assumed etymology of the name is fanciful. The Jehovist knew no Seth and the Elohist no Cain and Abel.

[II 4-IV]

In the day that the LORD God [Yahweh-Elohim] made earth and heaven, no plant of the field was yet in the earth, and no herb of the field had yet sprung up, for the LORD God had not caused it to rain upon the earth, and there was not a man to till the ground; but there went up a mist from the earth, and watered the whole face of the ground. And the LORD God formed man of the dust of the ground, and breathed into his nostrils the breath of life; and man became a living soul.

And the LORD God planted a garden eastward, in Eden; and there he put the man whom he had formed. And out of the ground made the LORD God to grow every tree that is pleasant to the sight, and good for food; the tree of life also in the midst of the garden, and the tree of the knowledge of good and evil.

[And a river goes out of Eden to water the garden; and from thence it is parted, and becomes four heads. The name of the first is Pishon: that is it which compasseth the whole land of Havilah, where there is gold; and the gold of that land is good; there is bdellium and the onyx stone. And the name of the second river is Gihon; the same is it that compasseth the whole land of Cush. And the name of the third river is Hiddekel; that is it which goeth in front of Assyria. And the fourth river is Euphrates.]

And the LORD God took the man, and put him into the garden of Eden to dress it and to keep it. And the LORD God commanded the man, saying, Of every tree of the garden thou mayest freely eat; but of the tree of the knowledge of good and evil, thou shalt not eat of it, for in the day that thou eatest thereof thou shalt surely die.

And the LORD God said, It is not good that the man should be alone; I will make him an help meet for him. And out of the ground the LORD God formed every beast of the field, and every fowl of the air; and brought them unto the man to see what he would call them; and whatsoever the man called every living creature, that was the name thereof. And the man gave names to all cattle, and to the fowl of the air, and to every beast of the field; but for man there was not found an help meet for him.

And the LORD God caused a deep sleep to fall upon the man, and he slept; and he took one of his ribs, and closed up the flesh in its place; and of the rib, which the LORD God had taken from the man, made he a woman, and brought her unto the man. And the man said, This is now bone of my bones, and flesh of my flesh; she shall be called Woman, because she was taken out of man. Therefore shall a man leave his father and his mother, and shall cleave unto his wife; and they shall be one flesh. And they were both naked, the man and his wife, and were not ashamed.

Now the serpent was more subtle than any beast of the field which the Lord God had made. And he said unto the woman, Yea, hath God said, Ye shall not eat of any tree of the garden? And the woman said unto the serpent, Of the fruit of the trees of the garden we may eat, but of the fruit of the tree which is in the midst of the garden, God hath said, Ye shall not eat of it, neither shall ye touch it, lest ye die. And the serpent said unto the woman, Ye shall not surely die, for God doth know that in the day ye eat thereof, then your eyes shall be opened, and ye shall be as God, knowing good and evil.

And when the woman saw that the tree was good for food, and that it was a delight to the eyes, and that the tree was to be desired to make one wise, she took of the fruit thereof, and did eat; and she gave also unto her husband with her, and he did eat. And the eyes of them both were opened, and they knew that they were naked; and they sewed fig leaves together, and made themselves girdles.

And they heard the sound of the Lord God walking in the garden in the cool of the day, and the man and his wife hid themselves from the presence of the Lord God amongst the trees of the garden. And the Lord God called unto the man, and said unto him, Where art thou? And he said, I heard thy footsteps in the garden, and I was afraid, because I was naked; and I hid myself. And he said, Who told thee that thou wast naked? Hast thou eaten of the tree, whereof I commanded thee that thou shouldest not eat? And the man said, The woman whom thou gavest to be with me, she gave me of the tree, and I did eat. And the LORD God said unto the woman, What is this thou hast done? And the woman said, The serpent beguiled me, and I did eat.

And the LORD God said unto the serpent, Because thou hast done this, cursed art thou above all cattle, and above every beast of the field; upon thy belly shalt thou go, and dust shalt thou eat all the days of thy life; and I will put enmity between thee and the woman, and between thy offspring and her offspring: it shall bruise thy head, and thou shalt bruise his heel. Unto the woman he said, I will greatly multiply thy pain and thy conception; in sorrow thou shalt bring forth children; and thy desire shall be to thy husband, and he shall rule over thee.

And unto Adam he said, Because thou hast hearkened unto the voice of thy wife, and hast eaten of the tree, of which I commanded thee, saying, Thou shalt not eat of it: cursed is the ground for thy sake; in toil shalt thou eat of it all the days of thy life; thorns also and thistles shall it bring forth to thee; and thou shalt eat the herb of the field; in the sweat of thy face shalt thou eat bread, till thou return unto the ground; for out of it wast thou taken: for dust thou art, and unto dust shalt thou return. [And the man called his wife's name

Eve; because she was the mother of all living.] And the LORD God made for Adam and for his wife coats of skins, and clothed them.

And the LORD God said, Behold, the man is become as one of us, to know good and evil; and now, lest he put forth his hand, and take also of the tree of life, and eat, and live for ever —

Therefore the LORD God sent him forth from the garden of Eden, to till the ground from whence he was taken. So he drove out the man; and he placed at the east of the garden of Eden the Cherubim, and the flame of a sword which turned every way, to keep the way of the tree of life.

And the man knew Eve his wife; and she conceived, and bare Cain, and said, I have gotten a man with the help of the LORD [Yahweh]. And again she bare his brother Abel. And Abel was a keeper of sheep, but Cain was a tiller of the ground. And in process of time it came to pass, that Cain brought of the fruit of the ground an offering unto the LORD. And Abel, he also brought of the firstlings of his flock and of the fat thereof. And the LORD had respect unto Abel and to his offering; but unto Cain and to his offering he had not respect. And Cain was very wroth, and his countenance fell.

And the LORD said unto Cain, Why art thou wroth? and why is thy countenance fallen? If thou doest well, shalt thou not be accepted? and if thou doest not well? — Sin coucheth at the door, and lieth in wait for thee, but thou shouldest rule over it. And Cain said unto Abel his brother —

And it came to pass, when they were in the field, that Cain rose up against Abel his brother, and slew him. And the LORD said unto Cain, Where is Abel thy brother? And he said, I know not; am I my brother's keeper? And he said, What hast thou done? The voice of thy brother's blood crieth unto me from the ground. And now cursed art thou from the ground, which hath opened her mouth to receive thy brother's blood from thy hand; when thou tillest the ground, it shall not henceforth yield unto thee her strength; a fugitive and a wanderer shalt thou be in the earth.

And Cain said unto the LORD, My punishment is greater than I can bear. Behold, thou hast driven me out this day from the face of the ground; and from thy face shall I be hid; and I shall be a fugitive and a wanderer in the earth; and it shall come to pass, that whosoever findeth me shall slay me. And the LORD said unto him, Therefore whosoever slayeth Cain, vengeance shall be taken on him sevenfold. And the LORD appointed a sign for Cain, lest any finding him should smite him. And Cain went out from the presence of the Lord, and dwelt in the land of Nod [wandering] in front of Eden.

And Cain knew his wife; and she conceived, and bare Enoch; and he builded a city, and called the name of the city, after the name of his son, Enoch. And unto Enoch was born Irad, and Irad begat

Mehujael, and Mehujael begat Methushael, and Methushael begat Lamech.

And Lamech took unto him two wives; the name of the one was Adah, and the name of the other Zillah. And Adah bare Jabal: he was the father of such as dwell in tents and *have* cattle. And his brother's name was Jubal: he was the father of all such as handle the harp and pipe. And Zillah, she also bare Tubal-cain, the forger of every cutting instrument of brass and iron; and the sister of Tubal-cain was Naamah. And Lamech said unto his wives:

> Adah and Zillah, hear my voice;
> Ye wives of Lamech, hearken unto my speech:
> For I have slain a man for wounding me,
> And a young man for bruising me:
> If Cain shall be avenged sevenfold,
> Truly Lamech seventy and sevenfold.

[And Adam knew his wife again; and she bare a son, and called his name Seth: For, said she, God hath appointed me another offspring instead of Abel; for Cain slew him. And to Seth, to him also there was born a son; and he called his name Enosh. Then began men to call upon the name of the LORD.]

III

THE ANTEDILUVIAN GENERATIONS

THE fifth chapter of Genesis is from the Elohist document and its close connection with the passage from the same source with which the book opens is quite obvious. While the reference to the creation of man, as male and female, in the plural, is repeated, the personification of the father of mankind in Adam is made definite in accordance with a plan which pervades the whole book. The Elohist was much given to genealogies personifying places and peoples. According to him there were ten antediluvian generations of long life. A distinct relation has been traced between the names of the heads of these generations with their durations, and those of the antediluvian dynasties of Chaldean legend, but it is no part of the present purpose to follow this out. The correspondence of the years of Enoch's age, after which he "walked with God" and "was not," with the number of days in the year is noticeable, and suggests an astronomical myth, of which the Chaldeans had many.

Lamech, the father of Noah, appears in the seventh generation after Seth, while the Jehovist made him the descendant of Cain in the fifth generation. The intermediate names in the two genealogies vary in their form and order, but evidently had a common source. The northern writer was less familiar with geographical and legendary appellations than the author of the Elohist document, and there was no system or direct purpose in his slight use of them.

[V]

This is the book of the generations of Adam. In the day that God [Elohim] created man, in the likeness of God made he him; male and female created he them; and blessed them, and called their name Adam [man], in the day when they were created. And Adam lived an hundred and thirty years, and begat a son in his own likeness, after his image, and called his name Seth; and the days of Adam after he begat Seth were eight hundred years, and he begat sons and daughters. And all the days that Adam lived were nine hundred and thirty years, and he died.

And Seth lived an hundred and five years, and begat Enosh; and Seth lived after he begat Enosh eight hundred and seven years, and begat sons and daughters; and all the days of Seth were nine hundred and twelve years, and he died.

And Enosh lived ninety years, and begat Kenan, and Enosh lived after he begat Kenan eight hundred and fifteen years, and begat sons and daughters; and all the days of Enosh were nine hundred and five years, and he died.

And Kenan lived seventy years, and begat Mahalalel; and Kenan lived after he begat Mahalalel eight hundred and forty years, and begat sons and daughters; and all the days of Kenan were nine hundred and ten years, and he died.

And Mahalalel lived sixty and five years, and begat Jared; and Mahalalel lived after he begat Jared eight hundred and thirty years, and begat sons and daughters; and all the days of Mahalalel were eight hundred ninety and five years, and he died.

And Jared lived an hundred sixty and two years, and begat Enoch; and Jared lived after he begat Enoch eight hundred years, and begat sons and daughters; and all the days of Jared were nine hundred sixty and two years, and he died.

And Enoch lived sixty and five years, and begat Methuselah; and Enoch walked with God after he begat Methuselah three hundred years, and begat sons and daughters; and all the days of Enoch were three hundred sixty and five years, and Enoch walked with God and he was not, for God took him.

And Methuselah lived an hundred eighty and seven years, and begat Lamech; and Methuselah lived after he begat Lamech seven hundred eighty and two years, and begat sons and daughters; and all the days of Methuselah were nine hundred sixty and nine years, and he died.

And Lamech lived an hundred eighty and two years, and begat a son, and he called his name Noah [saying, This same shall comfort us for our work and for the toil of our hands, because of the ground which the LORD hath cursed]. And Lamech lived after he begat Noah five hundred ninety and five years, and begat sons and daughters; and all the days of Lamech were seven hundred seventy and seven years, and he died.

And Noah was five hundred years old; and Noah begat Shem, Ham, and Japheth.

IV

THE MIXED ACCOUNT OF THE FLOOD

IN the old days when the memories of mankind first began to take form in myths and legends, which were ultimately preserved in writing, there seems to have been in the East a wide-spread tradition of a great cataclysm of nature, accompanied by an overwhelming flood of waters. It is not unlikely that this had come down from actual occurrences in the valleys of the great rivers, and on the shores of the seas some time in the early history of the human race. It is no more than natural if the inhabitants of regions in which this tradition prevailed, with their limited knowledge of the world's area, vastly exaggerated the extent of the destruction attending such catastrophes, and nothing could be more useful to the makers of myths than the terror they inspired.

The ancient Hebrews had no tradition of their own of this kind, but the Chaldeans of the Euphrates valley had one of the most highly developed of the diluvian myths, and it has been sufficiently traced to put beyond doubt that it furnished the material of the story of "Noah's Flood." The compiler adopted the Elohist version of this story, but interpolated in it some fragments and phrases from the other, which he seemed to regard as necessary to complete it, but which really confused it. If the passage given below, which constitutes the four chapters, vi.–ix., of the Book of Genesis, is read without the fragments that are bracketed or italicized, it will be found to be complete and harmonious in itself. It represents Noah as taking the animals into the ark two by two, male and female, for preservation, with no distinction of clean and unclean.

The Elohist, in his account of the creation, represented God as giving to man the "herb yielding seed," and the fruit of every tree to be "for food," and the "green herb" for food for animals. In preparing the ark for its perilous voyage Noah is directed to take two of every sort of living things "to keep them alive," and to gather "of all food that is eaten" for himself and for them. The same writer describes God as blessing Noah after the flood, and delivering into his hand the beast of the earth, the fowl of the air, and the fishes of the sea, and giving him "every moving thing that liveth" for food. This appears with him to be the origin of animal food for man. He represented the deluge of waters as the result of a general cataclysm, a breaking up of the fountains of the great deep, and an opening of the windows of heaven, and he allows a hundred and fifty days for the rise of the overwhelming flood, and a like period for its subsidence. He leaves Noah and his family in the ark more than a year. In the Chaldean legend there appears to have been an association of this period with an astronomical myth.

The other account, doubtless that of the Jehovist, represents Noah as taking seven pairs of "clean beasts" into the ark, the overplus beyond what was necessary for the preservation of species being presumably for food. The inadequacy of accommodations in the ark, as it is described, for what it was to contain, is a detail of no account, if we recognize the mythical character of the whole story. Such incongruities are common in antique fable. The writer, who had conceived of the earth at the creation as a barren waste of land waiting for moisture, instead of a chaos of waters from which the land was to emerge, conceived of the flood as the result of a steady down-pour of rain. According to him Noah entered the ark and waited seven days, and then the flood of waters came in a rainfall of forty days and forty nights, when it subsided, and the ark rested "upon the mountains of Ararat." To him belong the incidents of opening the window and sending out a raven and a dove, and finally looking forth and finding the face of the ground dried. The time of waiting on the mountain top was made up of three periods of seven days, and seventy days covered the whole time of the stay in the ark.

The difference in the two accounts of the flood, which the compiler mixed up, is plainly discernible when we separate the broken fragments of the one from the continuous fabric of the other. The passages and phrases which do not belong to the Elohist version are printed below in italics, those which were wrought into it as a part of the same narrative being put in brackets. At the beginning and at the end of the whole story are two separate interpolations which are bracketed and left in Roman type. The first is a curious bit of antique material with no direct relation to the context and is inconsistent with the post-diluvian genealogies in the decree of shortened life for man. The last shows Noah in a wholly different aspect from that of the story of the flood, and is apparently a scrap from the old patriarchal legends, introduced for the sake of the curse upon the people of Canaan, who were to be made subject to the offspring of Shem, from whom the Israelites were descended. It incidentally reflects a gross and sensual character imputed to the Southern races, or descendants of Ham, and rebukes a special form of disrespect for fathers. The statement of Noah's age which follows connects with the genealogy of Chapter v., and seems to have been broken off from it by the insertion of the story of the flood after the preliminary statement of his age when he "begat Shem, Ham and Japheth."

[VI-IX]

[And it came to pass, when men began to multiply on the face of the ground, and daughters were born unto them, that the sons of God saw the daughters of men that they were fair; and they took them wives of all that they chose. And the LORD said, My spirit shall not strive with man for ever, for that he also is flesh; yet shall his days be an hundred and twenty years. The Nephilim (giants) were in the earth in those days, and also after that, when the sons of God came in unto the daughters of men, and they bare children to them: the same were the mighty men which were of old, the men of renown.]

And the LORD *saw that the wickedness of man was great in the earth, and that every imagination of the thoughts of his heart was only evil continually.*

And it repented the LORD *that he had made man on the earth, and it grieved him at his heart. And the* LORD *said, I will destroy man whom I have created from the face of the ground; both man, and beast, and creeping thing, and fowl of the air; for it repenteth me that I have made them. But Noah found grace in the eyes of the* LORD.

These are the generations of Noah. Noah was a righteous man, and blameless in his generations. Noah walked with God. And Noah begat three sons, Shem, Ham, and Japheth. And the earth was corrupt before God, and the earth was filled with violence. And God saw the earth, and, behold, it was corrupt; for all flesh had corrupted his way upon the earth.

And God said unto Noah, The end of all flesh is come before me; for the earth is filled with violence through them; and, behold, I will destroy them with the earth. Make thee an ark of gopher wood; rooms shalt thou make in the ark, and shalt pitch it within and without with pitch. And this is how thou shalt make it: the length of the ark three hundred cubits, the breadth of it fifty cubits, and the height of it thirty cubits. A light shalt thou make to the ark, and to a cubit shalt thou finish it upward; and the door of the ark shalt thou set in the side thereof; with lower, second, and third stories shalt thou make it.

And I, behold, I do bring the flood of waters upon the earth, to destroy all flesh, wherein is the breath of life, from under heaven; every thing that is in the earth shall die. But I will establish my covenant with thee; and thou shalt come into the ark, thou, and thy sons, and thy wife, and thy sons' wives with thee. And of every living thing of all flesh, two of every sort shalt thou bring into the ark, to keep them alive with thee; they shall be male and female. Of the fowl after their kind, and of the cattle after their kind, of every creeping thing of the ground after its kind, two of every sort shall come unto thee, to keep them alive. And take thou unto thee of all food that is eaten, and gather it to thee; and it shall be for food for thee, and for them. Thus did Noah; according to all that God commanded him, so did he.

And the LORD *said unto Noah, Come thou and all thy house into the ark; for thee have I seen righteous before me in this generation. Of every clean beast thou shalt take to thee seven and seven, the male and his female; and of the beasts that are not clean two, the male and his female; of the fowl also of the air, seven and seven, male and female, to keep the race alive upon the face of all the earth. For yet seven days, and I will cause it to rain upon the earth forty days and forty nights; and every living thing that I have made will I destroy from off the face of the ground. And Noah did according unto all that the* LORD *commanded him.*

And Noah was six hundred years old when the flood of waters was upon the earth. And Noah went in, and his sons, and his wife, and his sons' wives with him, into the ark, because of the waters of the flood. Of [*clean*] beasts, [*and of beasts that are not clean,*] and of fowls, and of every thing that creepeth upon the ground, there went in two and two unto Noah into the ark, male and female, as God commanded Noah. [*And it came to pass after the seven days, that the waters of the flood were upon the earth.*]

In the six hundredth year of Noah's life, in the second month, on the seventeenth day of the month, on the same day were all the fountains of the great deep broken up, and the windows of heaven were opened. [*And the rain was upon the earth forty days and forty nights.*] In the selfsame day entered Noah, and Shem, and Ham, and Japheth, the sons of Noah, and Noah's wife, and the three wives of his sons with them, into the ark; they, and every beast after its kind, and all the cattle after their kind, and every creeping thing that creepeth upon the earth after its kind, and every fowl after its kind, every bird of every sort. And they went in unto Noah into the ark, two and two of all flesh wherein is the breath of life. And they that went in, went in male and female of all flesh, as God commanded him; [*and the* LORD *shut him in. And the flood was forty days upon the earth; and the waters increased, and bare up the ark, and it was lift up above the earth.*]

And the waters prevailed, and increased greatly upon the earth; and the ark went upon the face of the waters. And the waters prevailed exceedingly upon the earth; and all the high mountains that were under the whole heaven were covered. Fifteen cubits upward did the waters prevail; and the mountains were covered. And all flesh died that moved upon the earth, both fowl, and cattle, and beast, and every creeping thing that creepeth upon the earth, and every man : [*all in whose nostrils was the breath of the spirit of life, of all that was in the dry land, died. And every living thing was destroyed which was upon the face of the ground, both man, and cattle, and creeping thing, and fowl of the heaven; and they were destroyed from the earth; and Noah only was left, and they that were with him in the ark.*] And the waters prevailed upon the earth an hundred and fifty days.

And God remembered Noah, and every living thing, and all the cattle that were with him in the ark; and God made a wind to pass over the earth, and the waters assuaged; the fountains also of the deep and the windows of heaven were stopped; [*and the rain from heaven was restrained; and the waters returned from off the earth continually:*] and after the end of an hundred and fifty days the waters decreased [*and the ark rested*] in the seventh month, on the seventeenth day of the month [*upon the mountains of Ararat.*] And the waters decreased continually until the tenth month. In the tenth month, on the first day of the month, were the tops of the mountains seen.

[*And it came to pass at the end of forty days, that Noah opened the window of the ark which he had made; and he sent forth a raven, and it went forth to and fro, until the waters were dried up from off the earth. And he sent forth a dove from him, to see if the waters were abated from off the face of the ground; but the dove found no rest for the sole of her foot, and she returned unto him to the ark, for the waters were on the face of the whole earth; and he put forth his hand, and took her, and brought her in unto him into the ark. And he stayed yet other seven days; and again he sent forth the dove out of the ark; and the dove came in to him at eventide; and, lo, in her mouth an olive leaf pluckt off: so Noah knew that the waters were abated from off the earth. And he stayed yet other seven days; and sent forth the dove; and she returned not again unto him any more.*]

And it came to pass in the six hundred and first year, in the first month, the first day of the month, the waters were dried up from off the earth; [*and Noah removed the covering of the ark, and looked, and, behold, the face of the ground was dried.*] And in the second month, on the seven and twentieth day of the month, was the earth dry.

And God spake unto Noah, saying, Go forth of the ark, thou, and thy wife, and thy sons, and thy sons' wives with thee. Bring forth with thee every living thing that is with thee of all flesh, both fowl, and cattle, and every creeping thing that creepeth upon the earth; that they may breed abundantly in the earth, and be fruitful, and multiply upon the earth. And Noah went forth, and his sons, and his wife, and his sons' wives with him. Every beast, every creeping thing, and every fowl, whatsoever moveth upon the earth, after their families, went forth out of the ark.

And Noah builded an altar unto the LORD; and took of every clean beast, and of every clean fowl, and offered burnt offerings on the altar. And the LORD smelled the sweet savour; and the LORD said in his heart, I will not again curse the ground any more for man's sake, for that the imagination of man's heart is evil from his youth; neither will I again smite any more every thing living, as I have done. While the earth remaineth, seedtime and harvest, and cold and heat, and summer and winter, and day and night shall not cease.

And God blessed Noah and his sons, and said unto them, Be fruitful, and multiply, and replenish the earth. And the fear of you and the dread of you shall be upon every beast of the earth, and upon every fowl of the air; with all wherewith the ground teemeth, and all the fishes of the sea, into your hand are they delivered. Every moving thing that liveth shall be food for you; as the green herb have I given you all. But flesh with the life thereof, which is the blood thereof, shall ye not eat. And surely your blood, the blood of your lives, will I avenge; from every beast will I exact retribution for it; and at the hand of man, even at the hand of every man's brother, will I exact retribution for the life of man. Whoso sheddeth man's blood, by man shall his blood be shed, for in the image of God made he man. And you, be ye fruitful, and multiply; bring forth abundantly in the earth, and multiply therein.

And God spake unto Noah, and to his sons with him, saying, And I, behold, I establish my covenant with you, and with your posterity after you; and with every living creature that is with you, the fowl, the cattle, and every beast of the earth with you; of all that go out of the ark, even every beast of the earth. And I will establish my covenant with you; neither shall all flesh be cut off any more by the waters of the flood; neither shall there any more be a flood to destroy the earth.

And God said, This is the token of the covenant which I make between me and you and every living creature that is with you, for perpetual generations: I do set my bow in the cloud, and it shall be for a token of a covenant between me and the earth. And it shall come to pass, when I bring a cloud over the earth, that the bow shall be seen in the cloud, and I will remember my covenant, which is between me and you and every living creature of all flesh; and the waters shall no more become a flood to destroy all flesh. And the bow shall be in the cloud; and I will look upon it, that I may remember the everlasting covenant between God and every living creature of all flesh that is upon the earth. And God said unto Noah, This is the token of the covenant which I have established between me and all flesh that is upon the earth.

And the sons of Noah, that went forth of the ark, were Shem, and Ham, and Japheth: and Ham is the father of Canaan. These three were the sons of Noah: and of these was the whole earth overspread.

[And Noah began to be an husbandman, and planted a vineyard; and he drank of the wine, and was drunken, and he was uncovered within his tent. And Ham, the father of Canaan, saw the nakedness of his father, and told his two brethren without. And Shem and Japheth took a garment, and laid it upon both their shoulders, and went backward, and covered the nakedness of their father; and their faces were backward, and they saw not their father's nakedness. And Noah awoke from his wine, and knew what his youngest son had done unto him. And he said,

> Cursed be Canaan;
> A servant of servants shall he be unto his brethren.

And he said,

> Blessed be the LORD, the God of Shem;
> And let Canaan be his servant.
> God enlarge Japheth,
> And let him dwell in the tents of Shem;
> And let Canaan be his servant.]

And Noah lived after the flood three hundred and fifty years. And all the days of Noah were nine hundred and fifty years: and he died.

V

POST-DILUVIAN GENERATIONS

CHAPTER X. of the Book of Genesis is purely ethnographical and was intended to account for the distribution of population within the range of the writer's geography. Its basis was no doubt in the Elohist document, as a genealogy of the descendants of Noah, but it appears to have been expanded by the compiler to conform to a somewhat more definite knowledge in his day. The names were partly those of places, some cities and some broader territorial designations, and partly those of tribes or peoples.

Japheth, which implied vast extent, comprehended the Northern and Western peoples, of which comparatively little was then known. Magog was a term applied to the distant Scythians, and Javan included the Ionians. Dodanim seems to be identical with the Rodanim of the Book of Chronicles, and is supposed to mean the Rhodians. Ham, which implied a hot climate, comprehended the people of the South and the distant East, including Egypt under the name of Mizraim. The Canaanite tribes did not properly belong to this division, but to the Semitic race. They were remotely akin to the Israelites, but their subjection and the hereditary antipathy engendered by it led to placing them among the progeny of Ham and putting a special opprobrium upon their name. The reference to Nimrod and the founding of Nineveh was an interpolation derived from the prolific source of Chaldean myth, in which the mighty hunter was an astronomical figure corresponding to Orion. The phrase "before the Lord" is simply an intensive or superlative form of expression. Zidon is mentioned both as the son of Canaan and as a place on "the border of the Canaanite"; and the personal names for the tribes of Canaan did not go beyond Heth, the supposed ancestor of the Hittites.

Shem, meaning simply "name," implied the noble strain in the descendants of Noah. Arpachshad was the name of a place, Shelah signified "emigration," and Peleg "division." The ethnography is by no means systematic or clear, and there is a repetition of names. Sheba and Havilah are given both as descendants of Ham and of Shem. The former represented the people of Southern Arabia, who are supposed to have become the progenitors of the Nubians and Abyssinians. Uz and Jobab, which irresistibly suggest

Job and the land of Uz, appear again in the genealogies of Seir and Edom (Chapter xxxvi.). The whole scheme was a rough attempt at accounting for the origin of the nations "divided in the earth after the flood," according to the imperfect geographical knowledge of the writer, and the slight revision of the compiler probably produced the repetitions.

The compiler followed this with a fragment (xi. 1–9) bearing the distinct characteristics of the Jehovist, with his fondness for the fabulous in dealing with the perversities of man. The preceding genealogy distinctly implied a diversity of language in the division of the races, "after their tongues," as well as their families, but this fragment assumed "one speech" until it was "confounded" in consequence of a rash attempt to keep the people from being scattered over the earth, by building a tower which should reach heaven. This picturesque bit of mythism was undoubtedly suggested by the unfinished temple of Bel in "the land of Shinar," and the assumed derivation of its name from the Hebrew verb "to confound" was mere fancy. It really meant the gate (or the house) of Bel, the deity of the Babylonians, and had no etymological relation to "balal" or any other Hebrew word.

After this a characteristic piece of genealogy from the Elohist (xi. 10-32) was introduced, tracing the direct line of descent from Shem to Abram. Exactly what significance might be attached to the definite statement of the ages of the several begetters of these generations — ten in number like those before the flood — we cannot say, but they furnish the means, if any is necessary, for exposing the utterly unhistorical character of the whole scheme. It represents the time in which Abram lived as being only three to four centuries after the destruction of all mankind except one family, from which he was descended in the tenth generation. And yet in that brief period had grown up many nations scattered over a wide area, with their various "borders" and cities, and "the great City of" Nineveh had been long ago founded. We know now that still existing pyramids must have been built a thousand years before the time assigned to Abram by the Hebrews themselves, and their own account of his career implies antiquity in the "Chaldees," and the establishment, for an indefinite time, of the Kingdom of Egypt.

Apart from the absurdity of supposing that all the development implied in these narratives, and well ascertained from other sources, had taken place in three or four centuries of time, if we note that this genealogy itself would make Shem, the son of Noah, a survivor of Abraham by thirty-five years, and a living contemporary of Pharaoh, Abimelech, and the other potentates of their time, the assumption takes a ludicrous aspect. The subject can, however, be regarded seriously without being taken as even intended to be matter of fact.

The first eleven chapters of Genesis constitute a work by themselves, composite, irregular, and fragmentary, but forming a prelude to the mythical history of Israel's ancestry.

[X–XI]

Now these are the generations of the sons of Noah: Shem, Ham and Japheth; and unto them were sons born after the flood.

The sons of Japheth: Gomer, and Magog, and Madai, and Javan, and Tubal, and Meshech, and Tiras. And the sons of Gomer: Ashkenaz, and Riphath, and Togarmah. And the sons of Javan: Elishah, and Tarshish, Kittim, and Dodanim. Of these were the isles of the nations divided in their lands, every one after his tongue; after their families, in their nations.

And the sons of Ham: Cush, and Mizraim, and Put, and Canaan. And the sons of Cush: Seba, and Havilah, and Sabtah, and Raamah, and Sabteca; and the sons of Raamah: Sheba, and Dedan.

[And Cush begat Nimrod. He began to be a mighty one in the earth. He was a mighty hunter before the LORD; wherefore it is said, Like Nimrod a mighty hunter before the LORD. And the beginning of his kingdom was Babel, and Erech, and Accad, and Calneh, in the land of Shinar. Out of that land he went forth into Assyria, and builded Nineveh, and Rehoboth-Ir, and Calah, and Resen between Nineveh and Calah (the same is the great city).] And Mizraim begat Ludim, and Anamim, and Lehabim, and Naphtuhim, and Pathrusim, and Casluhim [whence went forth the Philistines], and Caphtorim.

And Canaan begat Zidon his first-born, and Heth, and the Jebusite, and the Amorite, and the Girgashite, and the Hivite, and the Arkite, and the Sinite, and the Arvadite, and the Zemarite, and the Hamathite; and afterward were the families of the Canaanite spread abroad. And the border of the Canaanite was from Zidon, as thou goest toward Gerar, unto Gaza; as thou goest toward Sodom and Gomorrah and Admah and Zeboiim, unto Lasha. These are the sons of Ham, after their families, after their tongues, in their lands, in their nations.

And unto Shem, the father of all the children of Eber, the elder brother of Japheth, to him also were children born. The sons of Shem: Elam, and Asshur, and Arpachshad, and Lud, and Aram. And the sons of Aram: Uz, and Hul, and Gether, and Mash. And Arpachshad begat Shelah, and Shelah begat Eber. And unto Eber were born two sons; the name of the one was Peleg, for in his days was the earth divided; and his brother's name was Joktan. And Joktan begat Almodad, and Sheleph, and Hazarmaveth, and Jerah; and Hadoram, and Uzal, and Diklah; and Obal, and Abimael, and Sheba; and Ophir, and Havilah, and Jobab: all these were the sons of Joktan. And their dwelling was from Mesha, as thou goest toward Sephar, the mountain of the east. These are the sons of Shem, after their families, after their tongues, in their lands, after their nations.

These are the families of the sons of Noah, after their generations, in their nations; and of these were the nations divided in the earth after the flood.

[And the whole earth was of one language and of one speech. And it came to pass, as they journeyed east, that they found a plain in the land of Shinar; and they dwelt there. And they said one to another, Go to, let us make brick, and burn them thoroughly. And they had brick for stone, and bitumen had they for mortar. And they said, Go to, let us build us a city, and a tower, whose top may reach unto heaven, to make us a name, lest we be scattered abroad upon the face of the whole earth.

And the LORD came down to see the city and the tower, which the children of men builded. And the LORD said, Behold, they are one people, and they have all one language; and this is what they begin to do, and now nothing will be withholden from them which they purpose to do. Go to, let us go down, and there confound their language, that they may not understand one another's speech.

So the LORD scattered them abroad from thence upon the face of all the earth, and they left off building the city. Therefore was the name of it called Babel; because the LORD did there confound the language of all the earth; and from thence did the LORD scatter them abroad upon the face of all the earth.]

These are the generations of Shem. Shem was an hundred years old, and begat Arpachshad two years after the flood; and Shem lived after he begat Arpachshad five hundred years, and begat sons and daughters.

And Arpachshad lived five and thirty years, and begat Shelah; and Arpachshad lived after he begat Shelah four hundred and three years, and begat sons and daughters.

And Shelah lived thirty years, and begat Eber; and Shelah lived after he begat Eber four hundred and three years, and begat sons and daughters.

And Eber lived four and thirty years, and begat Peleg; and Eber lived after he begat Peleg four hundred and thirty years, and begat sons and daughters.

And Peleg lived thirty years, and begat Reu; and Peleg lived after he begat Reu two hundred and nine years, and begat sons and daughters.

And Reu lived two and thirty years, and begat Serug; and Reu lived after he begat Serug two hundred and seven years, and begat sons and daughters.

And Serug lived thirty years, and begat Nahor; and Serug lived after he begat Nahor two hundred years, and begat sons and daughters.

And Nahor lived nine and twenty years, and begat Terah; and Nahor lived after he begat Terah an hundred and nineteen years, and begat sons and daughters.

And Terah lived seventy years, and begat Abram, Nahor, and Haran.

Now these are the generations of Terah. Terah begat Abram, Nahor, and Haran; and Haran begat Lot. And Haran died in the presence of his father Terah in the land of his nativity, in Ur of the Chaldees. And Abram and Nahor took them wives. The name of Abram's wife was Sarai; and the name of Nahor's wife, Milcah, the daughter of Haran, the father of Milcah, and the father of Iscah. And Sarai was barren; she had no child. And Terah took Abram his son, and Lot the son of Haran, his son's son, and Sarai his daughter in law, his son Abram's wife; and they went forth with them from Ur of the Chaldees, to go into the land of Canaan; and they came unto Haran, and dwelt there. And the days of Terah were two hundred and five years; and Terah died in Haran.

VI

ABRAHAM TAKES POSSESSION OF THE LAND

WITH Chapter xii. begins the story of Abraham, transformed from the mythical Chaldean king, father Orham, and from the putative ancestor of the kindred Semitic peoples, from the river to the sea, into the personal forefather of the Hebrew tribes. The different elements in this production are not so clearly distinguishable as those of the preceding section of the book, but there is plain evidence of their existence in the many inconsistencies of the narrative. The compiler wrought his materials together more completely, but not much more harmoniously, and the work of his own hand is more manifest. The Elohist document appears to have been rather meagre so far as it related to the Abraham legend, and the three episodes of Chapters xii. and xiii. are mainly from the Jehovist and derived by him largely from the original patriarchal idyls.

The first episode describes Abraham's departure from his own country to Shechem, where the land was promised to his progeny. The event was commemorated by building an altar, and then the possession of Bethel was consecrated by the same means. The passage in brackets is of different material from the rest and doubtless from the Elohist. Having taken possession of the North, Abraham journeyed south.

The second episode, beginning with xii. 11, is quite disconnected from this, and illustrates the divine favor supposed to be bestowed upon Abraham to protect him in a foreign land and to give him wealth. The device of a famine to account for his going into Egypt, and of plagues to explain his departure, was afterwards applied in a developed form in the case of his posterity. The incident of representing his wife to be his sister, as a means of protection to himself, throws light upon the moral ideas of the writer's time. There was no safeguard for the chastity of an unmarried woman, whether maid or widow, but any violation of the exclusive rights of the husband was regarded with horror. There appears to have been no sense of outrage if a sister should be appropriated for the harem of a sensual monarch, and Abraham is represented as being willing that his wife should meet the fate that might befall a sister to save himself from the fate of having her made a widow. The moral aspect of the case is somewhat mitigated by the fact that the writer was dealing with symbolical characters rather than real persons, but it nevertheless reflects the habit of thought of the time. Perhaps the æsthetic aspect of the case may also be relieved by the lack of reality in the characters; for the charms of Sarai must have been somewhat mature, as she was said to be sixty-five years of age when they left Haran.

The third episode (Chapter xiii.) explains the division of the land between Abraham, as the ancestor of Israel, and Lot, as the ancestor of Moab and Ammon, and the former's exclusive possession of the land of Canaan, albeit the "Canaanite and Perizzite" then dwelt there. There are traces of two diverse accounts of the division, one attributing it to the increase of the substance of the two chiefs, and the other to strife between their herdsmen. Notwithstanding all his wealth and substance in flocks and herds, the patriarch is described as passing through the land to revisit his altar at Bethel and as moving his tent to Hebron, the place which first became the centre of consecration for the Kingdom of Judah. This latter is apparently a touch from the Judean compiler, but the whole is in the true spirit of legend, typifying in a sweeping way the original occupation of the country. The interpolated statement as to the wickedness of Sodom appears to be the compiler's preparation for the story of its destruction introduced farther on.

[XII, XIII]

Now the LORD said unto Abram, Get thee out of thy country, and from thy kindred, and from thy father's house, unto the land that I will shew thee; and I will make of thee a great nation, and I will bless thee, and make thy name great; and be thou a blessing, and I will bless them that bless thee, and him that curseth thee will I curse, and in thee shall all the families of the earth be blessed.

So Abram went, as the LORD had spoken unto him; and Lot went with him: [and Abram was seventy and five years old when he departed out of Haran. And Abram took Sarai his wife, and Lot his brother's son, and all their substance that they had gathered, and the souls that they had gotten in Haran; and they went forth to go into the land of Canaan; and into the land of Canaan they came.]

And Abram passed through the land unto the place of Shechem, unto the oak of Moreh. And the Canaanite was then in the land. And the LORD appeared unto Abram, and said, Unto thy posterity will I give this land: and there builded he an altar unto the LORD, who appeared unto him. And he removed from thence unto the mountain on the east of Beth-el, and pitched his tent, having Beth-el on the west, and Ai on the east; and there he builded an altar unto the LORD, and called upon the name of the LORD.

And Abram journeyed, going on still toward the South; and there was a famine in the land, and Abram went down into Egypt to sojourn there, for the famine was sore in the land.

And it came to pass, when he was come near to enter into Egypt, that he said unto Sarai his wife, Behold now, I know that thou art a fair woman to look upon; and it shall come to pass, when the Egyptians shall see thee, that they shall say, This is his wife, and they will kill me, but they will save thee alive. Say, I pray thee, thou art my sister, that it may be well with me for thy sake, and that my soul may live because of thee.

And it came to pass, that, when Abram was come into Egypt, the Egyptians beheld the woman that she was very fair. And the princes of Pharaoh saw her, and praised her to Pharaoh; and the woman was taken into Pharaoh's house. And he dealt well with Abram for her sake; and he had sheep, and oxen, and he-asses, and menservants, and maidservants, and she-asses, and camels. And the LORD plagued Pharaoh and his house with great plagues because of Sarai Abram's wife. And Pharaoh called Abram, and said, What is this that thou hast done unto me? Why didst thou not tell me that she was thy wife? Why saidst thou, She is my sister, so that I took her to be my wife? Now therefore behold thy wife, take her, and go thy way. And Pharaoh gave men charge concerning him; and they brought him on the way, and his wife, and all that he had.

And Abram went up out of Egypt, he, and his wife, and all that he had, into the South, and Lot was with him. [And Abram was very rich in cattle, in silver, and in gold.] And he went on his journeys from the South even to Beth-el, unto the place where his tent had been at the beginning, between Beth-el and Ai; unto the place of the altar, which he had made there at the first; and there Abram called on the name of the LORD.

[And Lot also, which went with Abram, had flocks, and herds, and tents. And the land was not able to bear them, that they might dwell together, for their substance was great, so that they could not dwell together.] And there was a strife between the herdmen of Abram's cattle and the herdmen of Lot's cattle: [*and the Canaanite and the Perizzite dwelled then in the land.*] And Abram said unto Lot, Let there be no strife, I pray thee, between me and thee, and between my herdmen and thy herdmen; for we are brethren. Is not the whole land before thee? Separate thyself, I pray thee, from me; if thou wilt take the left hand, then I will go to the right; or if thou take the right hand, then I will go to the left.

And Lot lifted up his eyes, and beheld all the Plain of Jordan, that it was well watered every where before the LORD destroyed Sodom and Gomorrah, like the garden of the LORD, like the land of Egypt, as thou goest unto Zoar. So Lot chose him all the Plain of Jordan; and Lot journeyed east; [and they separated themselves the one from the other. Abram dwelled in the land of Canaan, and Lot dwelled in the cities of the Plain,] and moved his tent as far as Sodom. [*Now the men of Sodom were wicked and sinners against the Lord exceedingly.*]

And the Lord said unto Abram, after that Lot was separated from him, Lift up now thine eyes, and look from the place where thou art, northward and southward and eastward and westward; for all the land which thou seest, to thee will I give it, and to thy posterity for ever. And I will make thy race as the dust of the earth, so that if a man can number the dust of the earth, then shall thy race also be numbered. Arise, walk through the land in the length of it and in the breadth of it; for unto thee will I give it.

And Abram moved his tent, and came and dwelt by the terebinths of Mamre, which are in Hebron, and built there an altar unto the LORD.

VII

ABRAHAM AS A WARLIKE CHIEF

THE passage which stands apart as the fourteenth chapter of Genesis presents Abraham in a character and aspect that appear nowhere else. Whether the compiler found it as a legend complete in itself, or extracted it from some longer document, or whether he composed it from existing material, written or oral, with a purpose of his own, is matter only of conjecture. Most critics assume that it was contained in the Jehovist document, but two widely different views have been taken of it.

Some have regarded it as a fragment of ancient chronicle, revealing glimpses of an antique world in the light of reality, — a scene torn from a panorama of prehistoric life in the weird region of the Dead Sea. Others see in it a myth later than the main substance of the story rather than earlier, illustrating, like many another legend of the kind, the invincible might of the favorite of Israel's God as against the heathen. In support of this view is cited the extravagant improbability of the exploit of pursuing through the length and breadth of the land the armies of the confederated kings, with a band of three hundred and eighteen trained men "born in his house," and recovering their plunder. The use of the name "Damascus" was relatively modern, and Dan, at the northern border of the land, was established late in the period of the judges. Of the country devastated by the invading kings from the East was that of the Amalekites. In the ethnographical system of the book, the Amalekites were the descendants of Amalek, and in the eponymic genealogies of the Elohist, farther on, Amalek was the grandson of Abraham's grandson Esau.

These anachronisms appear inconsistent with the assumed antiquity of the composition, whatever may be said of the traditions from which it might have been derived. The vivid picture of Melchizedek, blessing Abraham, and receiving from him a tenth of all, is so different from all other references in Hebrew story to alien rulers and pagan priests, as to suggest a device for giving an ancient sanctity to Salem, the site of the Judean capital, to the union of the functions of king and priest in one person, and to the payment of tithes for the support of his beneficent sway. Moreover, the significance of the name,

"King of righteousness," would rather imply a symbolical character in the whole story than a recognition of superior sovereignty in an ancient Jebusite monarch on the height of Salem (peace). These suggestions, if they point to the truth, indicate a relatively late composition for this passage, though wrought upon an antique pattern. The term "El-Elion" (God most high) was in use in Phœnicia.

The writer of the letter to the Hebrews in the New Testament, erroneously credited to St. Paul in the canon, plainly regarded Melchizedek as an allegorical character, "being first, by interpretation, King of righteousness, and then also King of Salem, which is King of peace; without father, without mother, without genealogy, having neither beginning of days nor end of life, but made like unto the Son of God." Doubtless the whole story of the slaughter of the kings, and the giving of a tenth of all the recovered spoil to this king of righteousness and peace, was a symbolical representation of the power and sanctity of Israel's mythical ancestor, and of the obligation of his descendants to devote a tithe of their substance to the consecrated impersonation of an authority derived from the God of Abraham. One of the incidental touches which seem inconsistent with the special antiquity of this production is the prosaic statement that one who had escaped "told Abram the Hebrew." The word "Hebrew" did not come into use as a designation of the people of Israel until after the establishment of the kingdoms. The main features of the narrative were doubtless suggested by one of the many invasions of the Southern country from Shinar (Chaldea) and Elam (beyond the Tigris). The original author perhaps made use of real traditions and wove into them the exploits of Abraham.

[XIV]

And it came to pass in the days of Amraphel king of Shinar, Arioch king of Ellasar, Chedorlaomer king of Elam, and Tidal king of Goiim, that they made war with Bera king of Sodom, and with Birsha king of Gomorrah, Shinab king of Admah, and Shemeber king of Zeboiim, and the king of Bela [*the same is Zoar*]. All these joined together in the vale of Siddim [*the same is the Salt Sea*]. Twelve years they served Chedorlaomer, and in the thirteenth year they rebelled.

And in the fourteenth year came Chedorlaomer, and the kings that were with him, and smote the Rephaim in Ashteroth-karnaim, and the Zuzim in Ham, and the Emim in Shaveh-kiriathaim, and the Horites in their mount Seir, unto El-paran, which is by the wilderness. And they returned, and came to En-mishpat [*the same is Kadesh*], and smote all the country of the Amalekites, and also the Amorites, that dwelt in Hazazon-tamar. And there went out the king of Sodom, and the king of Gomorrah, and the king of Admah, and the king of Zeboiim, and the king of Bela [*the same is Zoar*]; and they set the battle in array against them in the vale of Siddim; against Chedorlaomer king of Elam, and Tidal king of Goiim, and Amraphel king of Shinar, and Arioch king of Ellasar; four kings against the five.

Now the vale of Siddim was full of bitumen pits; and the kings of Sodom and Gomorrah fled, and they fell there, and they that remained fled to the mountain. And they took all the goods of Sodom and Gomorrah, and all their victuals, and went their way. And they took Lot, Abram's brother's son, who dwelt in Sodom, and his goods, and departed. And there came one that had escaped, and told Abram the Hebrew. Now he dwelt by the oaks of Mamre the Amorite, brother of Eshcol, and brother of Aner; and these were confederate with Abram.

And when Abram heard that his brother was taken captive, he led forth his trained men, born in his house, three hundred and eighteen, and pursued as far as Dan. And he divided himself against them by night, he and his servants, and smote them, and pursued them unto Hobah, which is on the left hand of Damascus. And he brought back all the goods, and also brought again his brother Lot, and his goods, and the women also, and the people. And the king of Sodom went out to meet him, after his return from the slaughter of Chedorlaomer and the kings that were with him, at the vale of Shaveh [*the same is the King's Vale*].

And Melchizedek king of Salem brought forth bread and wine; and he was priest of God Most High [El-Elion]. And he blessed him, and said, Blessed be Abram of God Most High, maker of heaven and earth; and blessed be God Most High, which hath delivered thine enemies into thy hand. And he gave him a tenth of all.

And the king of Sodom said unto Abram, Give me the persons, and take the goods to thyself. And Abram said to the king of Sodom, I have lifted up mine hand unto the LORD, God Most High, maker of heaven and earth, that I will not take a thread nor a shoelatchet nor aught that is thine, lest thou shouldest say, I have made Abram rich; save only that which the young men have eaten, and the portion of the men who went with me, Aner, Eshcol, and Mamre, let them take their portion.

VIII

FIRST ACCOUNT OF THE COVENANT

CHAPTER XV. contains the Jehovist account of the original compact between Abraham and Jehovah, which appears to be made up from the most ancient material. It has a weird quality peculiar to itself,—in the word of the Lord coming in a vision, in the antique sacrifice as a ceremony in making a solemn covenant, in the prediction of Egyptian servitude and deliverance, and in the flame and smoke to indicate the presence of deity. It involves only the promise of the possession of the land to the posterity of Abraham, which is made more impressive by the not uncommon device of representing him as old and childless at the time. It will be observed that this version of the story brings Abraham himself and not his father Terah from "Ur of the Chaldees."

The fact that the reciprocal obligation of obedience does not appear, and no religious aspect is given to the transaction, leads one to believe that the account was part of the old material used by the Jehovist, rather than of his own composition. It is quite distinct from what precedes and follows, and the mythical quality is unusually marked. The promise of dominion from the "River of Egypt" to the Euphrates was according to the hope always cherished in Israel but never realized. The epithet "Dammesek," applied to Abraham's servant Eliezer, is commonly explained as meaning Damascene, but some learned Hebraists regard this as a misconception of the original. The phrase rendered by this word, "Dammesek," is said to be unusual but capable of signifying the son of property as distinguished from the son of the person, and therefore implying inheritance otherwise than by blood, where there is failure of offspring, in accordance with an ancient rule for the descent of property.

The opening phrase of this passage, "after these things," merely constitutes a connective expression, the equivalent of which was frequently used by the compiler in passing from one to another of the episodes culled from his varied material.

[XV]

After these things the word of the LORD came unto Abram in a vision, saying, Fear not, Abram; I am thy shield, and thy reward shall be exceeding great. And Abram said, O Lord God, what wilt thou give me, seeing I go childless, and he that shall be possessor of my house is Dammesek Eliezer? And Abram said, Behold, to me thou hast given no offspring; and, lo, one born in my house is mine heir.

And, behold, the word of the Lord came unto him, saying, This man shall not be thine heir; but he that shall come forth out of thine own bowels shall be thine heir. And he brought him forth abroad, and said, Look now toward heaven, and tell the stars, if thou be able to tell them: and he said unto him, So shall thy posterity be. And he believed in the Lord; and he counted it to him for righteousness.

And he said unto him, I am the Lord that brought thee out of Ur of the Chaldees, to give thee this land to inherit it. And he said, O Lord God, whereby shall I know that I shall inherit it? And he said unto him, Take me an heifer of three years old, and a she-goat of three years old, and a ram of three years old, and a turtledove, and a young pigeon. And he took him all these, and divided them in the midst, and laid each half over against the other; but the birds divided he not. And the birds of prey came down upon the carcases, and Abram drove them away. And when the sun was going down, a deep sleep fell upon Abram; and, lo, an horror of great darkness fell upon him.

And he said unto Abram, Know of a surety that

thy offspring shall be a stranger in a land that is not theirs, and shall serve them; and they shall afflict them four hundred years; and also that nation, whom they shall serve, will I judge; and afterward shall they come out with great substance. But thou shalt go to thy fathers in peace; thou shalt be buried in a good old age. And in the fourth generation they shall come hither again, for the iniquity of the Amorite is not yet full.

And it came to pass, that, when the sun went down, and it was dark, behold a smoking furnace, and a flaming torch that passed between these pieces. In that day the LORD made a covenant with Abram, saying, Unto thy race have I given this land, from the river of Egypt unto the great river, the river Euphrates: the Kenite, and the Kenizzite, and the Kadmonite, and the Hittite, and the Perizzite, and the Rephaim, and the Amorite, and the Canaanite, and the Girgashite, and the Jebusite.

IX

FIRST STORY OF HAGAR AND ISHMAEL

THE people of Arabia were known to be akin to those of Palestine, and to Israel they were known generally as Ishmael (God hears), or as Ishmaelites. Those who dwelt in Arabia Petræa were called "Hagrites," a term assumed to be from Hagar, meaning "flight," the same as Hegira. The significance of the names attached to places and to tribes and peoples usually contained the germs of the ethnic story evolved therefrom to account for the origin of such peoples and their possession of the places.

The Israelites acknowledged the common descent of the Ishmaelites from their great ancestor, but relegated them to an inferior relation with the story of the Egyptian handmaid and her son. The story seems to have had several forms. In that contained in the passage below (Genesis xvi.), the turning into the wilderness of the "wild ass among man" is represented as taking place in the person of the mother before the birth of the child, because she began to assume airs of superiority in consequence of her prospects. The use of the word "angel" in our English version, here and elsewhere, is apt to be misleading. The original (maleak) varies in its application, but frequently implies an apparition of the actual deity in a visible or audible manner. The name of the well, still existing in the writer's day, helped out the story, as it implied that one had there seen God and yet lived. The fragments in brackets are an interpolation from the Elohist document, which contained the Hagar story that comes later on (Chapter xxi.). It belongs to the same narrative with the fragment in Chapter xii., which says that Abram was seventy-five years old when he came to the land of Canaan.

[XVI]

Now Sarai, Abram's wife, bare him no children; and she had an handmaid, an Egyptian, whose name was Hagar. And Sarai said unto Abram, Behold now, the LORD hath restrained me from bearing; go in, I pray thee, unto my handmaid; it may be that I shall obtain children by her. And Abram hearkened to the voice of Sarai. [And Sarai Abram's wife took Hagar the Egyptian, her handmaid, after Abram had dwelt ten years in the land of Canaan, and gave her to Abram her husband to be his wife.] And he went in unto Hagar, and she conceived; and when she saw that she had conceived, her mistress was despised in her eyes.

And Sarai said unto Abram, My wrong be upon thee. I gave my handmaid into thy bosom; and when she saw that she had conceived, I was despised in her eyes. The LORD judge between me and thee. But Abram said unto Sarai, Behold, thy maid is in thy hand; do to her that which is good in thine eyes. And Sarai dealt hardly with her, and she fled from her face. And the angel of the LORD found her by a fountain of water in the wilderness, by the fountain in the way to Shur. And he said, Hagar, Sarai's handmaid, whence camest thou? and whither goest thou? And she said, I flee from the face of my mistress Sarai. And the angel of the LORD said unto her, Return to thy mistress, and submit thyself under her hands.

And the angel of the LORD said unto her, I will greatly multiply thy offspring, that it shall not be numbered for multitude. And the angel of the LORD said unto her, Behold, thou art with child, and shalt bear a son; and thou shalt call his name Ishmael, because the LORD hath heard thy affliction. And he shall be as a wild-ass among men; his hand shall be against every man, and every man's hand against him; and he shall dwell over against all his brethren.

And she called the name of the LORD that spake unto her, Thou art a God that seeth: for she said, Have I even here looked after him that seeth me? Wherefore the well was called Beerlahai-roi; behold, it is between Kadesh and Bered. [And Hagar bare Abram a son: and Abram called the name of his son, which Hagar bare, Ishmael. And Abram was fourscore and six years old, when Hagar bare Ishmael to Abram.]

I

X

THE ELOHIST ACCOUNT OF THE COVENANT

CHAPTER XVII. of Genesis is an extract, little, if at all, modified, from the document of the Elohist. It contains his account of the first compact with Abram, or Abraham, and is clearly distinguished from the other by its didactic and matter-of-fact quality. The Elohist was much given to exact forms of statement, as in giving the age of persons, the duration of periods of time, and the names of persons and places referred to. His conception of the covenant was of a promise on the part of God — Elohim, or El Shaddai — to give the land of Abraham's sojournings to his posterity, and to protect them in its possession; and in return they were to be devoted to the exclusive worship of this God.

The practice of the rite of circumcision was to be the token of fidelity to their pledge. The practice of circumcision was not original with the Hebrews, and it was not so old among them as this story would imply, but they were the first to make it a religious rite, and they adopted it as a pledge of their exclusiveness, probably because they brought it among a people who did not use it, and to whom it may have been repellent. The Elohist writer was connected with the early temple service, and he turned the covenant with Abraham to account to give a special sanction to the rite of circumcision, just as he had used the story of the creation to consecrate the observance of the Sabbath, which had become an equally sacred requirement in his eyes.

While there was a slight etymological difference of meaning between the two forms, Ab-ram and Abraham, from which the explanation of a change of name was evolved, they were in tradition merely variations in the designation of a mythical or legendary personage, one of which finally superseded the other and came into exclusive use. The same statement will apply to the change from Sarai to Sarah. While the definite promise of the son Isaac appears here first in the compiler's narrative, this is not its oldest form. Observe the difference in which the general promise of posterity is received here and in the ancient version of the covenant in Chapter xv. There we are solemnly assured, "he believed in the Lord," while here Abraham appears as sceptically laughing at the idea of having children when he is a hundred years old and his wife ninety.

The name "Isaac" for the promised child is derived from this laugh. The name seems really to have been adopted into the patriarchal legends as a link between the remote ancestor of all the Semitic nations and the special ancestor of the Israelites, from a tradition in the Beersheba region of an ancient tribe, Isaak-el, meaning "God laughs," or "laugh of God." The exact meaning of such epithets is a matter of inference from the words out of which they appear to be formed; and from the meaning so inferred, whether exact or not, the stories explaining their origin were evolved. Thus it happens that when two or more such stories have been preserved they are apt to be inconsistent. If they were not, the coincidence would be remarkable. Some significance may have been attached to making Abraham just a hundred years old when Isaac was born. In a vague, general way in the older story of the covenant a hundred years is made synonymous with a generation, as forty years was assumed to be in the later annals.

[XVII]

And when Abram was ninety years old and nine, the LORD appeared to Abram, and said unto him, I am God Almighty [El Shaddai]; walk before me, and be thou perfect. And I will make my covenant between me and thee, and will multiply thee exceedingly.

And Abram fell on his face; and God talked with him, saying, As for me, behold, my covenant is with thee, and thou shalt be the father of a multitude of nations. Neither shall thy name any more be called Abram, but thy name shall be Abraham; for the father of a multitude of nations have I made thee. And I will make thee exceeding fruitful, and I will make nations of thee, and kings shall come out of thee. And I will establish my covenant between me and thee and thy posterity throughout their generations for an everlasting covenant, to be a God unto thee and to thy posterity. And I will give unto thee, and to thy posterity, the land of thy sojournings, all the land of Canaan, for an everlasting possession; and I will be their God.

And God said unto Abraham, And as for thee, thou shalt keep my covenant, thou, and thy posterity throughout their generations. This is my covenant, which ye shall keep, between me and you and thy posterity; every male among you shall be circumcised. And ye shall be circumcised in the flesh of your foreskin; and it shall be a token of a covenant betwixt me and you. And he that is eight days old shall be circumcised among you, every male throughout your generations, he that is born in the house, or bought with money of any stranger, which is not of thy offspring. He that is born in thy house, and he that is bought with thy money, must needs be circumcised, and my covenant shall be in your flesh for an everlasting covenant. And the uncircumcised male who is not circumcised in the flesh of his foreskin, that soul shall be cut off from his people; he hath broken my covenant.

And God said unto Abraham, As for Sarai thy wife, thou shalt not call her name Sarai, but Sarah shall her name be. And I will bless her, and moreover I will give thee a son of her; yea, I will bless her, and she shall be a mother of nations; kings of people shall be of her. Then Abraham fell upon his face, and laughed, and said in his heart, Shall a child be born unto him that is an hundred years old? and shall Sarah, that is ninety years old, bear?

And Abraham said unto God, Oh that Ishmael might live before thee! And God said, Nay, but Sarah thy wife shall bear thee a son; and thou shalt call his name Isaac; and I will establish my covenant with him for an everlasting covenant for his seed after him. And as for Ishmael, I have heard thee; behold, I have blessed him, and will make him fruitful, and will multiply him exceedingly; twelve princes shall he beget, and I will make him a great nation. But my covenant will I establish with Isaac, which Sarah shall bear unto thee at this set time in the next year.

And he left off talking with him, and God went up from Abraham. And Abraham took Ishmael his son, and all that were born in his house, and all that were bought with his money, every male among the men of Abraham's house, and circumcised the flesh of their foreskin in the selfsame day, as God had said unto him. And Abraham was ninety years old and nine, when he was circumcised in the flesh of his foreskin. And Ishmael his son was thirteen years old, when he was circumcised in the flesh of his foreskin. In the selfsame day was Abraham circumcised, and Ishmael his son. And all the men of his house, those born in the house, and those bought with money of the stranger, were circumcised with him.

XI

ANOTHER VERSION OF THE PROMISE OF ISAAC

IMMEDIATELY following, in the first part of Chapter xviii., we have the Jehovist version of the promise of the birth of Isaac, which is not only older than the other, but evidently formed out of the most primitive material. In substance and quality, in the simple representation of "the Lord" as a man with two companions, hospitably entertained by the pastoral patriarch, and giving his assurances as one person to another, we have evidence of the myth in its most antique form; and the contrast with the Elohist account is so marked that the efforts of learned men to "harmonize" the two reflect upon the sanity of their learning. Here it is Sarah that laughs at the absurdity of a couple so "stricken in age" having offspring, and thereby furnishes the derivation of the name "Isaac."

[XVIII 1-15]

And the LORD appeared unto him by the oaks of Mamre, as he sat in the tent door in the heat of the day; and he lifted up his eyes and looked, and, lo, three men stood over against him; and when he saw them, he ran to meet them from the tent door, and bowed himself to the earth, and said, My lord, if now I have found favour in thy sight, pass not away, I pray thee, from thy servant; let now a little water be fetched, and wash your feet, and rest yourselves under the tree, and I will fetch a morsel of bread, and comfort ye your heart; after that ye shall pass on, forasmuch as ye are come to your servant. And they said, So do, as thou hast said.

And Abraham hastened into the tent unto Sarah, and said, Make ready quickly three measures of fine meal, knead it, and make cakes. And Abraham ran unto the herd, and fetched a calf tender and good, and gave it unto the servant; and he hastened to dress it. And he took butter, and milk, and the calf which he had dressed, and set it before them; and he stood by them under the tree, and they did eat. And they said unto him, Where is Sarah thy wife? And he said, Behold, in the tent. And he said, I will certainly return unto thee when the season cometh round; and, lo, Sarah thy wife shall have a son. And Sarah heard in the tent door, which was behind him.

Now Abraham and Sarah were old, and well stricken in age; it had ceased to be with Sarah after the manner of women. And Sarah laughed within herself, saying, After I am waxed old shall I have pleasure, my lord being old also? And the LORD said unto Abraham, Wherefore did Sarah laugh, saying, Shall I of a surety bear a child, who am old? Is any thing too hard for the LORD? At the set time I will return unto thee, when the season cometh round, and Sarah shall have a son. Then Sarah denied, saying, I laughed not; for she was afraid. And he said, Nay; but thou didst laugh.

XII

THE CITIES OF THE PLAIN AND THE FAMILY OF LOT

THE compiler followed this version of the promise of Isaac with the story of the destruction of the cities of the Dead Sea plain and an account of the family of Lot, regarded as the progenitor of the Moabites and Ammonites. In this passage the effect of the compiler's own hand in working over the material is more noticeable than in anything that precedes.

The narrative consists of three distinct parts, and the manner and spirit of the first indicate that it had a later origin than the rest. In it the menace of destruction to the sinful cities is used to exhibit Abraham in the character of a mediator between God and man to save the righteous from the fate decreed to the wicked, and "the Lord" is represented as recognizing the justice of his plea and as willing to endure the wickedness of the many for the sake of the few righteous. This formal bit of instruction, and the reference to the children of Abraham keeping "the way of the Lord to do justice and judgment," so little in consonance with the general tone of these narratives, suggest a relatively late origin for this passage, which may have been wrought out by the compiler without obliterating from his material the primitive conception of "the Lord" in the aspect of a "man" conversing familiarly with the personification of a "great and mighty nation."

At the end of this interview "the Lord" disappears, and his two companions proceed as "angels" to Sodom. This episode of the visit of the "angels" to rescue the family of Lot, and of the destruction of the doomed cities, bears the distinct characteristics of the Jehovist writer weaving together for his purposes the traditions, oral or written, that were at his command. He mingled together the legend of the destruction of the cities by fire and brimstone, which had grown out of the weird desolation and the evidences of ancient conflagration in that region, and the ethnic myth of Lot as the nephew of Abraham and the ancestor of the Moabites and Ammonites. The Jehovist took a gloomy view of the evil tendency of the human race and the disposition of its creator to destroy it, as we have already noticed, and in his use of old tales he readily accepted the peculiarly anthropomorphic idea of the deity which pervaded them, while the Elohist was much more vague in his references to the Almighty.

The picture of the moral condition of Sodom, which is incidentally brought out, is much like that of Gibeah in the Book of Judges, and the two descriptions were not far from contemporaneous. The morals and manners suggested were not unfamiliar to the early writers of Israel in their own country, and the story of Sodom may have been intended to convey a lesson and a warning directly to their own people in their own time. As the scenery and geological peculiarities about the "Dead Sea" gave rise to the legend of the destruction of the cities, so doubtless the saline deposits in columnar form suggested the weird touch about Lot's wife, the only one — unreal as it is — that gives any air of reality to such a person.

The brief fragment in brackets at the end of this passage is from the Elohist, and sums up the whole story in his characteristic way, so different from that of the imaginative author of the other document.

What follows, forming the third part of this episode, is the ethnic story in its oldest form, derived from the ancient patriarchal legends, from which the fragment about the drunkenness of Noah and the curse of Canaan was drawn. It has the peculiar mythological quality of those old tales. A relation has been traced between the name Lot and an ancient Egyptian designation of the people occupying the territory below the Jordan Valley. Doubtless the name still existed in tradition in the time of the first Hebrew writers. There was no doubt of the kinship between the tribes of Israel and the Moabites and Ammonites of that region, or Moab and Ammon, as they were called. But a keen hostility was felt toward them on account of old conflicts when the Israelites were struggling for the possession of the land of Canaan, and the marauding attacks to which they continued to be subject, especially from the Ammonites on their borders.

On account of this state of feeling the makers of the ethnic myths would not allow that Moab and Ammon were direct descendants of their great ancestor Abraham, and not only set them off on a collateral line, but gave them an incestuous origin, and covered the name of Lot and his daughters with obloquy. The purely mythological character of the story is sufficiently evident in the entire disregard of reality or probability in the gross picture it presents. The phrase "unto this day" also plainly indicates an imaginative dealing by the writer with a remote past. The grossness of the passage is much relieved when we consider that it was not to be understood as dealing with persons but with nations. The crude simplicity of primitive expression was free from any sense of indecency, but it would have been impossible in an age when the scene pictured would excite special aversion.

[XVIII 16-XIX]

And the men rose up from thence, and looked toward Sodom; and Abraham went with them to bring them on the way.

And the LORD said, Shall I hide from Abraham that which I do; seeing that Abraham shall surely become a great and mighty nation, and all the nations of the earth shall be blessed in him? For I have known him, to the end that he may command his children and his household after him, that they may keep the way of the LORD, to do righteousness and justice; to the end that the LORD may bring upon Abraham that which he hath spoken of him.

And the LORD said, Because the cry of Sodom and Gomorrah is great, and because their sin is very grievous; I will go down now, and see whether they have done altogether according to the cry of it, which is come unto me; and if not, I will know. And the men turned from thence, and went toward Sodom, but Abraham stood yet before the LORD. And Abraham drew near, and said, Wilt thou consume the righteous with the wicked? Peradventure there be fifty righteous within the city: wilt thou consume and not spare the place for the fifty righteous that are therein? That be far from thee to do after this manner, to slay the righteous with the wicked, that so the righteous should be as the wicked; that be far from thee: shall not the Judge of all the earth do right? And the LORD said, If I find in Sodom fifty righteous within the city, then I will spare all the place for their sake.

And Abraham answered and said, Behold now, I have taken upon me to speak unto the Lord, which am but dust and ashes; peradventure there shall lack five of the fifty righteous: wilt thou destroy all the city for lack of five? And he said, I will not destroy it, if I find there forty and five. And he spake unto him yet again, and said, Peradventure there shall be forty found there. And he said, I will not do it for the forty's sake. And he said, Oh let not the Lord be angry, and I will speak; peradventure there shall thirty be found there. And he said, I will not do it, if I find thirty there. And he said, Behold now, I have taken upon me to speak unto the Lord; peradventure there shall be twenty found there. And he said, I will not destroy it for the twenty's sake. And he said, Oh let not the Lord be angry, and I will speak yet but this once; peradventure ten shall be found there. And he said, I will not destroy it for the ten's sake.

And the LORD went his way, as soon as he had left communing with Abraham, and Abraham returned unto his place.

And the two angels came to Sodom at even; and Lot sat in the gate of Sodom, and Lot saw them, and rose up to meet them; and he bowed himself with his face to the earth; and he said, Behold now my lords, turn aside, I pray you, into your servant's house, and tarry all night, and wash your feet, and ye shall rise up early, and go on your way. And they said, Nay; but we will abide in the street all night. And he urged them greatly; and they turned in unto him, and entered into his house; and he made them a feast, and did bake unleavened bread, and they did eat.

But before they lay down, the men of the city, even the men of Sodom, compassed the house round, both young and old, all the people from every quarter; and they called unto Lot, and said unto him, Where are the men which came in to thee this night? Bring them out unto us, that we may know them.

And Lot went out unto them to the door, and shut the door after him. And he said, I pray you, my brethren, do not so wickedly. Behold now, I have two daughters which have not known man; let me, I pray you, bring them out unto you, and do ye to them as is good in your eyes; only unto these men do nothing; forasmuch as they are come under the shadow of my roof.

And they said, Stand back. And they said, This one fellow came in to sojourn, and he will needs be a judge; now will we deal worse with thee, than with them. And they pressed sore upon the man, even Lot, and drew near to break the door. But the men put forth their hand, and brought Lot into the house to them, and shut to the door. And they smote the men that were at the door of the house with blindness, both small and great, so that they wearied themselves to find the door.

And the men said unto Lot, Hast thou here any relative besides? Thy sons, and thy daughters, and whomsoever thou hast in the city, bring them out of the place, for we will destroy this place, because the cry of them is waxen great before the LORD; and the LORD hath sent us to destroy it. And Lot went out, and spake unto his sons in law, which married his daughters, and said, Up, get you out of this place; for the LORD will destroy the city. But he seemed unto his sons in law as one that mocked.

And when the morning arose, then the angels hastened Lot, saying, Arise, take thy wife, and thy two daughters which are here; lest thou be consumed in the iniquity of the city. But he lingered; and the men laid hold upon his hand, and upon the hand of his wife, and upon the hand of his two daughters, the LORD being merciful unto him, and they brought him forth, and set him without the city.

And it came to pass, when they had brought them forth abroad, that he said, Escape for thy life; look not behind thee, neither stay thou in all the Plain; escape to the mountain, lest thou be consumed. And Lot said unto them, Oh, not so, my lord; behold now, thy servant hath found grace in thy sight, and thou hast magnified thy mercy, which thou hast shewed unto me in saving my life; and I cannot escape to the mountain, lest evil overtake me, and I die. Behold now, this city is near to flee unto, and it is a little one. Oh, let me escape thither, (is it not a little one?) and my soul shall live. And he said unto him, See, I have accepted thee concerning this thing also, that I will not overthrow the city of which thou hast spoken. Haste thee, escape thither; for I cannot do any thing till thou be come thither. Therefore the name of the city was called Zoar.

The sun was risen upon the earth when Lot came unto Zoar. Then the LORD rained upon Sodom and upon Gomorrah brimstone and fire from the LORD out of heaven; and he overthrew those cities, and all the Plain, and all the inhabitants of the cities, and that which grew upon the ground. But his wife looked back from behind him, and she became a pillar of salt.

And Abraham gat up early in the morning to the place where he had stood before the LORD; and he looked toward Sodom and Gomorrah, and toward all the land of the Plain, and beheld, and, lo, the smoke of the land went up as the smoke of a furnace.

[And it came to pass, when God destroyed the cities of the Plain, that God remembered Abraham, and sent Lot out of the midst of the overthrow, when he overthrew the cities in the which Lot dwelt.]

[And Lot went up out of Zoar, and dwelt in the mountain, and his two daughters with him, for he feared to dwell in Zoar; and he dwelt in a cave, he and his two daughters. And the firstborn said unto the younger, Our father is old, and there is not a man in the land to come in unto us after the manner of all the earth; come, let us make our father drink wine, and we will lie with him, that we may preserve the family of our father. And they made their father drink wine that night; and the firstborn went in, and lay with her father, and he knew not when she lay down, nor when she arose. And it came to pass on the morrow, that the firstborn said unto the younger, Behold, I lay yesternight with my father; let us make him drink wine this night also, and go thou in, and lie with him, that we may preserve offspring of our father. And they made their father drink wine that night also; and the younger arose, and lay with him, and he knew not when she lay down, nor when she arose. Thus were both the daughters of Lot with child by their father. And the firstborn bare a son, and called his name Moab; the same is the father of the Moabites unto this day. And the younger, she also bare a son, and called his name Ben-ammi; the same is the father of the children of Ammon unto this day.]

XIII

ABRAHAM AND ABIMELECH

THE compiler appears to have had in his material two episodes, associating Abraham with a Philistine king in the South, which were contained in neither of his two main documents. One of these he introduced immediately after the story of the cities of the plain and the family of Lot, where it now stands as Chapter xx. of the Book of Genesis, and the other he appended incongruously to the second version of the story of Hagar, where it constitutes the last part of Chapter xxi. There are traces of material in other parts of the book from what appears to be the same source. This material is designated by some critics as that of the "second Elohist," but it appears only in fragments and is older rather than later than the rest. It cannot be attributed to any particular writer or production, but was apparently drawn from the floating mass of primitive story.

The first episode with Abimelech is introduced by the compiler with the vague statement, "And Abraham journeyed from thence toward the land of the South." The account of the relations of Sarah and the King of Gerar is an obvious variant of that in Chapter xii. in regard to Sarah and Pharaoh; and it appears still more incongruous in this place from the fact that Sarah has already been represented as ninety years old, and as treating with derision the idea that she was capable of having children at that age. The story has no chronological relation, however, to other events, save in the arrangement of the compiler's narrative.

The explanatory sentence at the end, in brackets, is apparently the compiler's own, and he seems to have misconceived the nature of the penalty inflicted upon Abimelech and his people, which was evidently a general malady, or impotence, and not merely a barrenness of women. The story reflects again the moral ideas of the time of the writer. Abraham is represented as seriously telling Abimelech that Sarah was the daughter of his father, though at the end of Chapter xi. she is spoken of as Terah's daughter-in-law, not his daughter. This is incidental evidence, if any were needed, of diversity of origin in the two statements. The marriage of half-brothers and sisters, non-uterine in the relationship, was not regarded as illegitimate at the time of David and later, though finally interdicted in the Levitical law. It is to be observed that Abraham, in explaining his migration from his own country, says that God caused him to wander from his father's house, and there is no intimation of what is called his "vocation." In fact, this older material always appears to be devoid of the religious quality of the later.

[XX]

And Abraham journeyed from thence toward the land of the South, and dwelt between Kadesh and Shur; and he sojourned in Gerar. And Abraham said of Sarah his wife, She is my sister; and Abimelech king of Gerar sent, and took Sarah. But God came to Abimelech in a dream of the night, and said to him, Behold, thou art but a dead man, because of the woman which thou hast taken; for she is a man's wife. Now Abimelech had not come near her; and he said, Lord, wilt thou slay even a righteous nation? Said he not himself unto me, She is my sister? and she, even she herself said, He is my brother. In the integrity of my heart and the innocency of my hands have I done this. And God said unto him in the dream, Yea, I know that in the integrity of thy heart thou hast done this, and I also withheld thee from sinning against me; therefore suffered I thee not to touch her. Now therefore restore the man's wife; for he is a prophet, and he shall pray for thee, and thou shalt live; and if thou restore her not, know thou that thou shalt surely die, thou, and all that are thine.

And Abimelech rose early in the morning, and called all his servants, and told all these things in their ears; and the men were sore afraid. Then Abimelech called Abraham, and said unto him, What hast thou done unto us? and wherein have I sinned against thee, that thou hast brought on me and on my kingdom a great sin? Thou hast done deeds unto me that ought not to be done. And Abimelech said unto Abraham, What sawest thou, that thou hast done this thing? And Abraham said, Because I thought, Surely the fear of God is not in this place; and they will slay me for my wife's sake. And moreover she is indeed my sister, the daughter of my father, but not the daughter of my mother, and she became my wife; and it came to pass, when God caused me to wander from my father's house, that I said unto her, This is thy kindness which thou shalt shew unto me; at every place whither we shall come, say of me, He is my brother.

And Abimelech took sheep and oxen, and menservants and womenservants, and gave them unto Abraham, and restored him Sarah his wife. And Abimelech said, Behold, my land is before thee; dwell where it pleaseth thee. And unto Sarah he said, Behold, I have given thy brother a thousand pieces of silver; behold, it is for thee a covering of the eyes to all that are with thee, and in respect of all thou art righted. And Abraham prayed unto

God; and God healed Abimelech, and his wife, and his maidservants; and they bare children. [For the LORD had fast closed up all the wombs of the house of Abimelech, because of Sarah, Abraham's wife.]

XIV

SECOND STORY OF HAGAR AND HER SON

THE opening statement of Genesis xxi., which is put in brackets below, relating to the birth of Isaac, is from the Elohist document and immediately sequent upon the promise in Chapter xvii. The repetition in the first sentence may be due to the compiler starting off with his own language and then taking in the extract without change. What follows is mainly a version of the ethnic myth of Ishmael, as the ancestor of the people of the desert, quite different from that of the Jehovist in Chapter xvi. It is regarded as belonging to the material which has been infelicitously called the "second Elohist document," but which is merely foreign to the two main sources from which the compiler drew.

It begins with still another explanation of the meaning of the name "Isaac" (laughter), — the general merriment that such an old person as Sarah should have a child. But the main purpose of the story is to account for the alienation and separation of the earlier progeny of Abraham from the later. The Jehovist accounted for this by the expulsion of the Egyptian mother before the birth of the child, on account of her show of pride to the vexation of Sarah, while this writer attributed it to the scorn of the boy himself exhibited at Isaac's weaning, and to Sarah's jealousy of his becoming co-heir with her offspring. Abraham appears more sympathetic in this story than in the other, though his alleged treatment of the bondwoman and her child would be regarded in any but a mythical tale as cruel, since it would mean certain death by starvation in the wilderness for mother and child.

It is noticeable that in this version of the story the name of Ishmael is not mentioned, though the phrase derived from it, "God heard," is twice used. Where Ishmael is mentioned in the real Elohist material there is no intimation at all of an alienation from his father or mother, or of his expulsion to the wilderness. From that material it would appear that Hagar's son must have been a lad of about fifteen at the time of Isaac's weaning, while the story under consideration treats him as still a child whom his mother carries upon her shoulder and casts under a shrub. It also disposes of him finally as dwelling in the wilderness of Pharan with a wife taken for him out of Egypt by his mother, though we find him again in Chapter xxv. joining with Isaac in the burial of his father. The latter incident is evidently taken from the version of the story which did not recognize the expulsion of the Ishmaelites from the house of Abraham. The purely mythical quality of the following passage seems sufficiently manifest in its lack of all relation to reality or probability. It is also devoid of the religious trace which characterizes both the Jehovist and Elohist writers, except as an allegorical representation of the division of the people destined to divine favor from others of the same blood who were to be excluded from the heritage.

[XXI 1-21]

[*And the* LORD *visited Sarah as he had said*, and the LORD did unto Sarah as he had spoken. And Sarah conceived, and bare Abraham a son in his old age, at the set time of which God had spoken to him. And Abraham called the name of his son that was born unto him, whom Sarah bare to him, Isaac. And Abraham circumcised his son Isaac when he was eight days old, as God had commanded him. And Abraham was an hundred years old, when his son Isaac was born unto him.]

And Sarah said, God hath made me to laugh; every one that heareth will laugh with me. And

SECOND STORY OF HAGAR AND HER SON

she said, Who would have said unto Abraham, that Sarah should give children suck? for I have borne him a son in his old age.

And the child grew, and was weaned; and Abraham made a great feast on the day that Isaac was weaned. And Sarah saw the son of Hagar the Egyptian, which she had borne unto Abraham, mocking. Wherefore she said unto Abraham, Cast out this bondwoman and her son, for the son of this bondwoman shall not be heir with my son, even with Isaac.

And the thing was very grievous in Abraham's sight on account of his son. And God said unto Abraham, Let it not be grievous in thy sight because of the lad, and because of thy bondwoman; in all that Sarah saith unto thee, hearken unto her voice, for in Isaac shall thy progeny be called. And also of the son of the bondwoman will I make a nation, because he is thy offspring.

And Abraham rose up early in the morning, and took bread and a bottle of water, and gave it unto Hagar, putting it on her shoulder, and the child, and sent her away; and she departed, and wandered in the wilderness of Beersheba. And the water in the bottle was spent, and she cast the child under one of the shrubs. And she went, and sat her down over against him a good way off, as it were a bowshot; for she said, Let me not look upon the death of the child. And she sat over against him, and lifted up her voice, and wept.

And God heard the voice of the lad; and the

angel of God called to Hagar out of heaven, and said unto her, What aileth thee, Hagar? fear not; for God hath heard the voice of the lad where he is. Arise, lift up the lad, and hold him in thine hand; for I will make him a great nation. And God opened her eyes, and she saw a well of water; and she went, and filled the bottle with water, and gave the lad drink.

And God was with the lad, and he grew; and he dwelt in the wilderness, and became an archer. And he dwelt in the wilderness of Pharan; and his mother took him a wife out of the land of Egypt.

XV

COMPACT BETWEEN ABRAHAM AND ABIMELECH

THE second Abimelech episode follows here quite irrelevantly, the abrupt transition being made by the compiler with the words, "and it came to pass at that time," as the other story was brought in with the statement that "Abraham journeyed thence," etc. There had long been an ancient fane at Beersheba, on the southern border of the land of Israel, and the purpose of the original narrator was to account for its possession, and to connect its first consecration with Abraham, who was said to have planted the tamarisk tree which doubtless still marked the site of the old place of worship.

Beersheba meant the seven wells or the well of seven, but a mystic significance was attached to the number seven, and it was associated with treaties and solemn oaths, and the name was accounted for in the story by an agreement between Abraham and Abimelech for the possession of the place by the former, witnessed by the gift of seven ewe lambs. This story probably originated at a time of peace with the Philistines, after the conquests of David, and was incidently meant to cement friendly relations with those people by reference to an ancient compact of amity. The original Elohist writer, or, we may say, the real Elohist, always fixes the residence of Abraham at Hebron. It was the Jehovist, or the writer from whom his material was drawn, that associated him with Beersheba. The compiler, a "Jehovist" so far as the use of the name of the deity was concerned, and a Judean, writing after the Northern Kingdom had passed away, produced much incongruity in his narrative by trying to retain both traditions as to Abraham's place of residence.

[XXI 22-34]

And it came to pass at that time, that Abimelech and Phicol the captain of his host spake unto Abraham, saying, God is with thee in all that thou doest; now therefore swear unto me here by God that thou wilt not deal falsely with me, nor with my son, nor with my son's son; but according to the kindness that I have done unto thee, thou shalt do unto me, and to the land wherein thou hast sojourned. And Abraham said, I will swear.

And Abraham reproved Abimelech because of the well of water, which Abimelech's servants had violently taken away. And Abimelech said, I know not who hath done this thing; neither didst thou tell me, neither yet heard I of it, but to-day. And Abraham took sheep and oxen, and gave them unto Abimelech; and they two made a covenant. And Abraham set seven ewe lambs of the flock by themselves. And Abimelech said unto Abraham, What mean these seven ewe lambs which thou hast set by themselves? And he said, These seven ewe lambs shalt thou take of my hand, that it may be a witness unto me, that I have digged this well. Wherefore he called that place Beersheba; because there they sware both of them.

So they made a covenant at Beersheba; and Abimelech rose up, and Phicol the captain of his host, and they returned into the land of the Philistines. And Abraham planted a tamarisk tree in Beersheba, and called there on the name of the LORD, the Everlasting God. And Abraham sojourned in the land of the Philistines many days.

L

XVI

THE STORY OF OFFERING ISAAC

The material which forms the basis of the ethical episode in Chapter xxii. is as foreign to the main substance of the compiler's narrative as the warlike episode in Chapter xiv. The aspect in which it presents the aged patriarch, wandering for three days across the country with an ass laden with wood, and his child and two attendants, is in the broadest contrast with the warrior chieftain sweeping through the length of the land in pursuit of invading armies. The difference is due to the diversity of purpose in the two tales and furnishes the best evidence of the allegorical character of both.

This story, written after the temple had been established on Mount Moriah, and when one of the evil tendencies against which its teachers still had to strive was the sacrifice of children to the deity of whom the people stood in so much dread, had the double purpose of carrying the consecration of the "Mount of the Lord" back to Abraham, and of sanctifying the substitution of the firstlings of the flock for the first-born of the family as a burnt offering. The ancient offering of the first-born among all the people of that region to their gods, which seems to us so barbarous, merely testifies to the terrible character of their conceptions of the deity and the awful fear under which they performed their acts of worship. While human sacrifice excited an intense aversion in the Hebrews, they were not free from the sentiments which inspired it, and comparatively late in the history of the Kingdoms they were liable to lapse into this most appalling rite of their "heathen" neighbors. While the modern spirit revolts even against the bloody sacrifice and burnt offering of animals as a means of worship, it was surely a beneficent substitute for what it displaced.

This simple story of Abraham about to offer Isaac at God's command and being stayed by the "angel," so completely in the ancient Hebrew manner of conveying a lesson, was calculated to give an impressive sanction to animal sacrifice and to the prohibition of human sacrifice. The main story, comprising the first section of the passage below, is of the original material, introduced by the compiler with the familiar formula, "and it came to pass after these things," and was perhaps revised by him in the transcription. It is the compiler himself who takes occasion to connect with the story a repetition of the promise to Abraham as a reward for his obedience. He also assumes that Abraham was dwelling then at Beersheba, which does not so appear in the story itself.

This passage contains another significant example of the use of the word "maleak," of which the translation through the Greek of "angel" is apt to be misleading. It appears distinctly as an embodiment or personification of the deity himself, and even when it is represented as a separate person, or messenger, it seems to be an added or multiplied embodiment, a vestige of the polytheistic notion of the Elohim and Beni-elohim (Sons of God).

The ethnographic fragment at the end of the chapter relates back to the close of Chapter xi., and prepares the way for the coming story of Rebekah. It is curious to observe in it the common system of twelve tribes, of which four are of inferior blood, as the offspring of concubines. The names are mostly those of places, including that of Nahor, and the compiler brought in the fragment with the improbable statement that "it was told to Abraham"; but when we accept the mythical meaning of these representations they have no proper relation to probability.

[XXII]

And it came to pass after these things, that God did prove Abraham, and said unto him, Abraham! And he said, Here am I. And he said, Take now thy son, thine only son, whom thou lovest, even Isaac, and get thee into the land of Moriah; and offer him there for a burnt offering upon one of the mountains which I will tell thee of.

And Abraham rose early in the morning, and saddled his ass, and took two of his young men with him, and Isaac his son; and he clave the wood for the burnt offering, and rose up, and went unto the place of which God had told him. On the third day Abraham lifted up his eyes, and saw the place afar off. And Abraham said unto his young men, Abide ye here with the ass, and I and the lad will go yonder; and we will worship, and come again to you.

And Abraham took the wood of the burnt offering, and laid it upon Isaac his son; and he took in his hand the fire and the knife; and they went both of them together. And Isaac spake unto Abraham his father, and said, My father! And he said, Here am I, my son. And he said, Behold, the fire and the wood; but where is the lamb for a burnt offering? And Abraham said, God will provide himself the lamb for a burnt offering, my son; so they went both of them together.

And they came to the place which God had told him of; and Abraham built the altar there, and laid the wood in order, and bound Isaac his son, and laid him on the altar, upon the wood. And Abraham stretched forth his hand, and took the knife to slay his son. And the angel of the LORD called unto him out of heaven, and said, Abraham, Abraham! And he said, Here am I. And he said, Lay not thine hand upon the lad, neither do thou any thing unto him; for now I know that thou fearest God, seeing thou hast not withheld thy son, thine only son, from me.

And Abraham lifted up his eyes, and looked, and behold, behind him a ram caught in the thicket by his horns; and Abraham went and took the ram, and offered him up for a burnt offering in the stead of his son.

And Abraham called the name of that place Jehovah-jireh, as it is said to this day, In the mount of the LORD it shall be provided. And the angel of the LORD called unto Abraham a second time out of heaven, and saith, By myself have I sworn, saith the LORD, because thou hast done this thing, and hast not withheld thy son, thine only son, that in blessing I will bless thee, and in multiplying I will multiply thy progeny as the stars of the heaven, and as the sand which is upon the sea shore; and thy posterity shall possess the gate of his enemies;

and in thy posterity shall all the nations of the earth be blessed, because thou hast obeyed my voice.

So Abraham returned unto his young men, and they rose up and went together to Beersheba; and Abraham dwelt at Beersheba.

And it came to pass after these things, that it was told Abraham, saying, Behold, Milcah, she also hath borne children unto thy brother Nahor; Uz his firstborn, and Buz his brother, and Kemuel the father of Aram; and Chesed, and Hazo, and Pildash, and Jidlaph, and Bethuel. And Bethuel begat Rebekah. These eight did Milcah bear to Nahor, Abraham's brother. And his concubine, whose name was Reumah, she also bare Tebah, and Gaham, and Tahash, and Maacah.

XVII

THE SACRED BURIAL PLACE

BEFORE bringing in the Jehovist's story of the marriage of Isaac and Rebekah, the compiler introduced from the Elohist an account of the consecration of Hebron as the ancestral burial place. The story of the death of Sarah, and the purchase of the field of Machpelah is in the matter-of-fact style characteristic of the Elohist writer. Much stress is laid upon the acquisition of the land, by formal purchase, with the consent of the Hittites, for the highest consecration of Israel's right of possession in Canaan was the burial there of the ancestors of the race. The Elohist always associated Abraham with Hebron, the first sacred place of the Kingdom of Judah, and the compiler of the record saw that his bones and those of Isaac and Jacob were gathered to the original burial place of Sarah, to complete the consecration, though the developed story of Jacob, being that of the Jehovist, connected his name chiefly with the Northern Kingdom, and implied his final burial at or near Shechem.

[XXIII]

And the life of Sarah was an hundred and seven and twenty years: these were the years of the life of Sarah. And Sarah died in Kiriath-arba (the same is Hebron), in the land of Canaan; and Abraham came to mourn for Sarah, and to weep for her.

And Abraham rose up from before his dead, and spake unto the children of Heth, saying, I am a stranger and a sojourner with you; give me a possession of a buryingplace with you, that I may bury my dead out of my sight.

And the children of Heth answered Abraham, saying unto him, Hear us, my lord; thou art a prince of God among us; in the choice of our sepulchres bury thy dead; none of us shall withhold from thee his sepulchre, but that thou mayest bury thy dead.

And Abraham rose up, and bowed himself to the people of the land, even to the children of Heth. And he communed with them, saying, If it be your mind that I should bury my dead out of my sight, hear me, and intreat for me to Ephron the son of Zohar, that he may give me the cave of Machpelah, which he hath, which is in the end of his field; for the full price let him give it to me in the midst of you for a possession of a buryingplace.

Now Ephron was sitting in the midst of the children of Heth; and Ephron the Hittite answered Abraham in the audience of the children of Heth, even of all that went in at the gate of his city, saying, Nay, my lord, hear me; the field give I thee, and the cave that is therein, I give it thee; in the presence of the sons of my people give I it thee; bury thy dead.

And Abraham bowed himself down before the people of the land. And he spake unto Ephron in the audience of the people of the land, saying, But if thou wilt, I pray thee, hear me; I will give the price of the field; take it of me, and I will bury my dead there.

And Ephron answered Abraham, saying unto him, My lord, hearken unto me; a piece of land worth four hundred shekels of silver, what is that betwixt me and thee? bury therefore thy dead.

And Abraham hearkened unto Ephron; and Abraham weighed to Ephron the silver, which he had named in the audience of the children of Heth, four hundred shekels of silver, current money with the merchant. So the field of Ephron, which was in Machpelah, which was before Mamre, the field, and the cave which was therein, and all the trees that were in the field, that were in all the border thereof round about, were made sure unto Abraham for a possession in the presence of the children of Heth, before all that went in at the gate of his city.

And after this, Abraham buried Sarah his wife in the cave of the field of Machpelah before Mamre (the same is Hebron), in the land of Canaan. And the field, and the cave that is therein, were made sure unto Abraham for a possession of a buryingplace by the children of Heth.

XVIII

THE STORY OF REBEKAH

THE beautiful idyl which pictures the patriarchal caravan making its way over the hill country of Ephraim to Syria to bring back the bride of Isaac, bears all the marks of the imaginative genius of the Jehovist writer, as well as his habitual recognition of divine direction in whatever relates to the history of his people. The color is doubtless that of his own time, in the reign of Jehu, at Samaria, when relations with Damascus were somewhat familiar.

The story of antique kinship breathes kindliness between the two nations, which were prone to alternate quarrel and alliance, and there is a charming picture of Oriental hospitality in the camels kneeling at the well, the Syrian maiden with her water jar upon her shoulder welcoming the messenger from her father's wandering kinsmen in a distant land, the gifts of nose ring and bracelets, and of jewels and raiment, the eating and drinking and tarrying all night, and the parting benediction to the sister as she rode away on the gay trappings of the sleekest camel to her new home in a far country.

The purpose of the story appears in the introductory passage. Abraham, "old, and well stricken in age," contemplating the end of his eventful life, is anxious that his son shall not marry of the daughters of the Canaanites, and shall not himself go to "Aram of the two rivers" for a wife, lest he remain there and lose the heritage of his adopted land. Thus is poetically expressed at once the repeated injunction against intermarriage with "the people of the land," and a renewed sanction of its permanent possession. There is at the beginning no intimation of Abraham's place of abode, and we bring from the previous chapter an impression of Hebron, but the end carries us back to the South as the home of Isaac. But at that time there is no more question of the aged father. He has disappeared from the scene, and "the master" is now the son, who takes the bride to the tent of his mother, Sarah, whom we have seen buried at Hebron.

The mixed impression produced is due to the difference of origin of the stories of Sarah's death and of Isaac's marriage, and it was the compiler who added the prosaic close of the latter for the sake of completeness, and he was, fortunately, never at much pains to harmonize the material which he strung together with so little regard for continuity or consistency.

[XXIV]

And Abraham was old, and well stricken in age; and the LORD had blessed Abraham in all things. And Abraham said unto his servant, the elder of his house, that ruled over all that he had, Put, I pray thee, thy hand under my thigh; and I will make thee swear by the LORD, the God of heaven and the God of the earth, that thou shalt not take a wife for my son of the daughters of the Canaanites, among whom I dwell; but thou shalt go unto my country, and to my kindred, and take a wife for my son Isaac.

And the servant said unto him, Peradventure the woman will not be willing to follow me unto this land; must I needs bring thy son again unto the land from whence thou camest? And Abraham said unto him, Beware that thou bring not my son thither again. The LORD, the God of heaven, that took me from my father's house, and from the land of my nativity, and that spake unto me, and that sware unto me, saying, Unto thy offspring will I give this land, he shall send his messenger before thee, and thou shalt take a wife for my son from thence. And if the woman be not willing to follow thee, then thou shalt be clear from this my oath; only thou shalt not bring my son thither again. And the servant put his hand under the thigh of Abraham his master, and swear to him concerning this matter.

And the servant took ten camels, of the camels of his master, and departed, having all goodly things of his master's in his keeping; and he arose, and went to Mesopotamia, unto the city of Nahor. And he made the camels to kneel down without the city by the well of water at the time of evening, the time that women go out to draw water.

And he said, O Lord, the God of my master Abraham, send me, I pray thee, good speed this day, and shew kindness unto my master Abraham. Behold, I stand by the fountain of water; and the daughters of the men of the city come out to draw water; and let it come to pass, that the damsel to whom I shall say, Let down thy pitcher, I pray thee, that I may drink; and she shall say, Drink, and I will give thy camels drink also: let the same be she that thou hast appointed for thy servant Isaac; and thereby shall I know that thou has shewed kindness unto my master.

And it came to pass, before he had done speaking, that, behold, Rebekah came out, who was born to Bethuel the son of Milcah, the wife of Nahor, Abraham's brother, with her water jar upon her shoulder. And the damsel was very fair to look upon, a virgin, neither had any man known her; and she went down to the fountain, and filled her jar, and came up. And the servant ran to meet her, and said, Give me to drink, I pray thee, a little water of thy jar. And she said, Drink, my lord; and she hasted, and let down her jar upon her hand, and gave him drink. And when she had done giving him drink, she said, I will draw for thy camels also, until they have done drinking. And she hasted, and emptied her jar into the trough, and ran again unto the well to draw, and drew for all his camels.

And the man looked stedfastly on her; holding his peace, to know whether the LORD had made his journey prosperous or not. And it came to pass, as the camels had done drinking, that the man took a golden nose ring of half a shekel weight, and two bracelets for her hands of ten shekels weight of gold; and said, Whose daughter art thou? tell me, I pray thee. Is there room in thy father's house for us to lodge in? And she said unto him, I am the daughter of Bethuel the son of Milcah, which she bare unto Nahor. She said moreover unto him, We have both straw and provender enough, and room to lodge in.

And the man bowed his head, and worshipped the LORD. And he said, Blessed be the LORD, the God of my master Abraham, who hath not forsaken his mercy and his truth toward my master; as for me, the LORD hath led me in the way to the house of my master's brethren.

And the damsel ran, and told her mother's house according to these words. And Rebekah had a brother, and his name was Laban; and Laban ran out unto the man, unto the fountain. And it came to pass, when he saw the nose ring, and the bracelets upon his sister's hands, and when he heard the words of Rebekah his sister, saying, Thus spake the man unto me; that he came unto the man, and, behold, he stood by the camels at the fountain. And he said, Come in, thou blessed of the Lord; wherefore standest thou without? for I have prepared the house, and room for the camels.

And the man came into the house, and he ungirded the camels; and he gave straw and provender for the camels, and water to wash his feet and the men's feet that were with him. And there was set meat before him to eat; but he said, I will not eat, until I have told mine errand. And he said, Speak on.

And he said, I am Abraham's servant. And the Lord hath blessed my master greatly, and he is become great; and he hath given him flocks and herds, and silver and gold, and menservants and maidservants, and camels and asses. And Sarah my master's wife bare a son to my master when she was old, and unto him hath he given all that he hath. And my master made me swear, saying, Thou shalt not take a wife for my son of the daughters of the Canaanites, in whose land I dwell; but thou shalt go unto my father's house, and to my kindred, and take a wife for my son. And I said unto my master, Peradventure the woman will not follow me. And he said unto me, The Lord, before whom I walk, will send his messenger with thee, and prosper thy way; and thou shalt take a wife for my son of my kindred, and of my father's house; then shalt thou be clear from my oath, when thou comest to my kindred; and if they give her not to thee, thou shalt be clear from my oath. And I came this day unto the fountain, and said, O LORD, the God of my master Abraham, if now thou do prosper my way which I go: behold, I stand by the fountain of water; and let it come to pass, that the maiden which cometh forth to draw, to whom I shall say, Give me, I pray thee, a little water of thy water jar to drink; and she shall say to me, Both drink thou, and I will also draw for thy camels: let the same be the woman whom the LORD hath appointed for my master's son. And before I had done speaking in mine heart, behold, Rebekah came forth with her water jar on her shoulder; and she went down unto the fountain, and drew; and I said unto her, Let me drink, I pray thee. And she made haste, and let down her jar from her shoulder, and said, Drink, and I will give thy camels drink also; so I drank, and she made the camels drink also. And I asked her, and said, Whose daughter art thou? And she said, The daughter of Bethuel, Nahor's son, whom Milcah bare unto him; and I put the ring upon her nose, and the bracelets upon her hands. And I bowed my head, and worshipped the LORD, and blessed the LORD, the God of my master Abraham, which had led me in the right way to take my master's brother's daughter for his son. And now if ye will deal kindly and truly with my master, tell me; and if not, tell me; that I may turn to the right hand, or to the left.

M

Then Laban and Bethuel answered and said, The thing proceedeth from the LORD; we cannot speak unto thee bad or good. Behold, Rebekah is before thee, take her, and go, and let her be thy master's son's wife, as the LORD hath spoken.

And it came to pass, that, when Abraham's servant heard their words, he bowed himself down to the earth unto the LORD. And the servant brought forth jewels of silver, and jewels of gold, and raiment, and gave them to Rebekah; he gave also to her brother and to her mother precious things. And they did eat and drink, he and the men that were with him, and tarried all night; and they rose up in the morning, and he said, Send me away unto my master.

And her brother and her mother said, Let the damsel abide with us a few days, at the least ten; after that she shall go. And he said unto them, Hinder me not, seeing the LORD hath prospered my way; send me away that I may go to my master. And they said, We will call the damsel, and inquire at her mouth. And they called Rebekah, and said unto her, Wilt thou go with this man? And she said, I will go. And they sent away Rebekah their sister, and her nurse, and Abraham's servant, and his men. And they blessed Rebekah, and said unto her, Our sister, be thou the mother of thousands of ten thousands, and let thy offspring possess the gate of those which hate them. And Rebekah arose, and her damsels, and they rode upon the camels, and followed the man.

[And the servant took Rebekah, and went his way. And Isaac came from the way of Beer-lahai-roi; (for he dwelt in the land of the South.) And Isaac went out to meditate in the field at the eventide; and he lifted up his eyes, and saw, and, behold, there were camels coming. And Rebekah lifted up her eyes, and when she saw Isaac, she lighted off the camel. And she said unto the servant, What man is this that walketh in the field to meet us? And the servant said, It is my master; and she took her veil, and covered herself. And the servant told Isaac all the things that he had done. And Isaac brought her into his mother Sarah's tent, and took Rebekah, and she became his wife; and he loved her, and Isaac was comforted after his mother's death.]

XIX

VARIED PROGENY OF ABRAHAM

The compiler's disregard of consistency is strikingly illustrated in what immediately follows the story of Rebekah. Abraham had been represented as stricken in age and apparently about to die, and then had disappeared from the story. We gather from fragments of the Elohist document in the general narrative that Abraham was a hundred years old when Isaac was born, and it was then regarded as a marvel that he and his aged wife should be blessed with a son. It was thirty-seven years later when Sarah died, and Isaac was forty years old when he took Rebekah to be his wife. And yet another ethnographic fragment is brought in which represents Abraham as marrying again and having six children by his new wife Keturah, besides an unmentioned number of "sons of the concubines."

The names of the sons of Keturah are eponymic, and the fragment contains an independent attempt to account for the wandering tribes of the desert, inconsistent with that which represented them as the descendants of Ishmael.

Medan and Midian are variations of the same designation, and it will be noticed hereafter in the story of Joseph how the Midianites and Ishmaelites were confounded. In the account of Gideon's victory over Midian in the Book of Judges it is said that his captives had nose rings "because they were Ishmaelites."

Sheba and Dedan are designations of territory, the latter in the East, and the former in Southern Arabia and the upper Nile region, and both names appear in the post-diluvian ethnography of Chapter x. among the descendants of Ham. All this goes to show not only the mythical quality of this kind of material, but the diversity of its sources. This fragment could not have belonged to either of the documents containing the stories of Ishmael, and it seems to be wholly apart from the patriarchal tales.

The short passage which follows it, relating to the death and burial of Abraham, is unquestionably from the Elohist, who never separated Ishmael from his father's family, and who seldom fails to mention the age of his characters. He was much addicted to the details of family genealogy. The final statement of Isaac's residence in the South was evidently interpolated by the compiler.

The brief account of the "generations of Ishmael," which indicates again the system of twelve tribes, must be in substance at least from the Elohist, but the final statement is drawn from the Jehovist's story, being a mere repetition of xvi. 12.

This entire Chapter xxv. is made up by piecing together fragments from different materials in the hands of the compiler. After the Ishmaelite genealogy there is the beginning of the "generations of Isaac" from the Elohist document, but it is broken off to bring in the ethnic myth of Jacob and Esau, which is derived from the Jehovist, and probably belonged to his original material of the legends of the patriarchs.

When these were written, the Edomites had been brought into subjection by Israel, but it was a recognized fact that they were not only a kindred nation, but a much older one in the possession of a regular government. It suited the purpose of the writer to represent them as an uncivilized people over whom the Israelites had gained a primacy by their superior craft and thrift. The name "Edom" meant red and was applied to the people, while their country was generally called "Seir," which meant shaggy, or hairy. The Hebrew equivalent, "Esau," also meant hairy. In this primitive tale redness is not only attributed to the newly born child, but to the pottage for which he afterwards sold his birthright.

Jacob had long been a poetical designation of all Israel, and the name had an etymological relation to a word meaning heel. Out of these elements of the significance of names, the recognized relations of the two peoples, and the desire to exalt the origin of the one at the expense of the other, was developed this little myth in whose simplicity there is a depth of ethnic meaning characteristic of the productions of pristine genius.

[XXV]

[And Abraham took another wife, and her name was Keturah. And she bare him Zimran, and Jokshan, and Medan, and Midian, and Ishbak, and Shuah. And Jokshan begat Sheba, and Dedan. And the sons of Dedan were Asshurim, and Letushim, and Leummim. And the sons of Midian; Ephah and Epher and Hanoch, and Abida, and Eldaah. All these were the children of Keturah. And Abraham gave all that he had unto Isaac. But unto the sons of the concubines, which Abraham had, Abraham gave gifts; and he sent them away from Isaac his son, while he yet lived, eastward, unto the east country.]

And these are the days of the years of Abraham's life which he lived, an hundred threescore and fifteen years. And Abraham gave up the ghost, and died in a good old age, an old man, and full of years; and was gathered to his people. And Isaac and Ishmael his sons buried him in the cave of Machpelah, in the field of Ephron the son of Zohar the Hittite, which is before Mamre, the field which Abraham purchased of the children of Heth; there was Abraham buried, and Sarah his wife. And it came to pass after the death of Abraham, that God blessed Isaac his son; [*and Isaac dwelt by Beer-lahai-roi.*]

Now these are the generations of Ishmael, Abraham's son, whom Hagar the Egyptian, Sarah's handmaid, bare unto Abraham; and these are the names of the sons of Ishmael, by their names, according to their generations: the firstborn of Ishmael, Nebaioth; and Kedar, and Adbeel, and Mibsam, and Mishma, and Dumah, and Massa; Hadad, and Tema, Jetur, Naphish, and Kedemah: these are the sons of Ishmael, and these are their names, by their villages, and by their encampments, twelve princes according to their nations. And these are the years of the life of Ishmael, an hundred and thirty and seven years; and he gave up the ghost and died, and was gathered unto his people. [And they dwelt from Havilah unto Shur that is before Egypt, as thou goest toward Assyria: *he abode in the presence of all his brethren.*]

[And these are the generations of Isaac, Abraham's son: Abraham begat Isaac; and Isaac was forty years old when he took Rebekah, the daughter of Bethuel the Syrian of Paddan-aram, the sister of Laban the Syrian, to be his wife.] —

And Isaac intreated the LORD for his wife, because she was barren; and the LORD was intreated of him, and Rebekah his wife conceived. And the children struggled together within her; and she said, If it be so, wherefore do I live? And she went to inquire of the LORD. And the LORD said unto her,

> Two nations are in thy womb,
> And two peoples shall be separated
>   even from thy bowels;
> And the one people shall be stronger
>   than the other people;
> And the elder shall serve the younger.

And when her days to be delivered were fulfilled, behold, there were twins in her womb. And the first came forth red, all over like an hairy garment; and they called his name Esau. And after that came forth his brother, and his hand had hold on Esau's heel; and his name was called Jacob: [*and Isaac was threescore years old when she bare them.*]

And the boys grew; and Esau was a cunning hunter, a man of the field; and Jacob was a plain man, dwelling in tents. Now Isaac loved Esau, because he did eat of his venison; and Rebekah loved Jacob. And Jacob boiled pottage, and Esau came in from the field, and he was faint; and Esau said to Jacob, Feed me, I pray thee, with that same red pottage, for I am faint : therefore was his name called Edom. And Jacob said, Sell me this day thy birthright. And Esau said, Behold, I am at the point to die; and what profit shall the birthright do to me? And Jacob said, Swear to me this day; and he sware unto him, and he sold his birthright unto Jacob. And Jacob gave Esau bread and pottage of lentils; and he did eat and drink, and rose up, and went his way; so Esau despised his birthright.

XX

ISAAC AND ABIMELECH

WHILE the original traditions associated with Beersheba and the southern border of Philistia pertained to the name Isaac, which stood for some ancient branch of the Hebrew people in that region, they were freely used in the Abraham legend, and when the compiler of the narrative in the Book of Genesis came to deal with Isaac as a personality after his father's death, he used substantially the same material over again, or material drawn from the same traditions. There is scarcely anything in Chapter xxvi. which is not a repetition or variation of what was related of Abraham.

The material is in the main that of the Jehovist, who gave the account of Abraham's going to Egypt, in Chapter xii., but who had no hand in the story of Abraham and Abimelech in Chapter xx. The handiwork of the compiler himself is however more than usually evident. If we were to give heed to the apparent chronology of the record, we should note that since the first patriarch's sojourn at Gerar Isaac had been born and had reached the age of sixty at the birth of the two sons who have already been represented as grown up, and yet we find there the same King Abimelech and the same Phicol captain of his host. Practically the same story is told of the mother of the grown-up twins that was told of Sarah when she was ninety years old, and even then it was a variant of the tale of the fascination of Pharaoh at the time of the visit to Egypt a quarter of a century earlier. But chronology has nothing to do with material of this kind, which is drawn from various sources and used for different purposes without any relation to historical fact.

In this story, while the familiar device of a famine is used to account for a migration, Isaac is warned against going into Egypt. The main purpose is to illustrate the ancient relation with the Philistines of the South, a peaceable establishment of the division of territory with them, and the consecration of Beersheba as an Israelite possession and sacred place. The original writer apparently knew nothing of the other story, attributing this to Abraham, and the compiler, in his desire to give prominence to Isaac as an important link in the line of descent and of inheritance, retained both accounts. It was doubtless he who reiterated in the case of Isaac the promises made to Abraham. The repetition of the wife and sister story indicates barrenness of invention and seems quite unnecessary to the purpose in hand.

The statement of Isaac's prosperity is like that of Abraham's state aforetime, but there is evidence of the blending of two accounts of his differences with the Philistines and of their settlement. From one it would appear that the Philistines endeavored to check his encroachments by filling up his wells and cutting off the supply of water for his herds, and that the King of Gerar induced him to depart. The other represents him as opening the same wells, filled up long before, and his herdsmen as being still in contention with those of Gerar. All this is preliminary to taking possession of Beersheba, and entering into the treaty of peace with Abimelech from which the name of the place was derived. We are indebted to the compiler for retaining the inconsistent accounts which he found in his material of this and of other events, for it is precisely these variations, repetitions, and inconsistencies that have enabled students to trace, not with clearness perhaps, but with certainty, the different sources of his material, and to demonstrate the seriously mythical character and purpose of these old writings.

[XXVI 1-33]

And there was a famine in the land, beside the first famine that was in the days of Abraham. And Isaac went unto Abimelech king of the Philistines unto Gerar. And the LORD appeared unto him, and said, Go not down into Egypt; dwell in the land which I shall tell thee of; sojourn in this land, and I will be with thee, and will bless thee; for unto thee, and unto thy race, I will give all these lands, and I will establish the oath which I sware unto Abraham thy father; and I will multiply thy progeny as the stars of heaven, and will give unto thy posterity all these lands; and in thy posterity shall all the nations of the earth be blessed, because that Abraham obeyed my voice, and kept my charge, my commandments, my statutes, and my laws.

And Isaac dwelt in Gerar; and the men of the place asked him of his wife, and he said, She is my sister; for he feared to say, My wife, lest, said he, the men of the place should kill me for Rebekah: because she was fair to look upon.

And it came to pass, when he had been there a long time, that Abimelech king of the Philistines looked out at a window, and saw, and, behold, Isaac was caressing Rebekah his wife. And Abimelech called Isaac, and said, Behold, of a surety she is thy wife, and how saidst thou, She is my sister? And Isaac said unto him, Because I said, Lest I die for her. And Abimelech said, What is this thou hast done unto us? One of the people might lightly have lain with thy wife, and thou shouldest have brought guiltiness upon us. And Abimelech charged all the people, saying, He that toucheth this man or his wife shall surely be put to death.

And Isaac sowed in that land, and found in the same year an hundredfold; and the LORD blessed him. And the man waxed great, and grew more and more until he became very great; and he had possessions of flocks, and possessions of herds, and a great household, and the Philistines envied him. Now all the wells which his father's servants had digged in the days of Abraham his father, the Philistines had stopped them, and filled them with earth. And Abimelech said unto Isaac, Go from us, for thou art much mightier than we. And Isaac departed thence, and encamped in the valley of Gerar, and dwelt there.

[And Isaac digged again the wells of water, which they had digged in the days of Abraham his father; for the Philistines had stopped them after the death of Abraham; and he called their names after the names by which his father had called them.]

And Isaac's servants digged in the valley, and found there a well of springing water. And the herdmen of Gerar strove with Isaac's herdmen, saying, The water is ours; and he called the name of the well Esek, because they contended with him. And they digged another well, and they strove for that also; and he called the name of it Sitnah. And he removed from thence, and digged another well;

and for that they strove not, and he called the name of it Rehoboth; and he said, For now the LORD hath made room for us, and we shall be fruitful in the land.

And he went up from thence to Beersheba. And the LORD appeared unto him the same night, and said, I am the God of Abraham thy father; fear not, for I am with thee, and will bless thee, and multiply thy progeny for my servant Abraham's sake. And he builded an altar there, and called upon the name of the LORD, and pitched his tent there; and there Isaac's servants digged a well.

Then Abimelech went to him from Gerar, and Ahuzzath his friend, and Phicol the captain of his host. And Isaac said unto them, Wherefore are ye come unto me, seeing ye hate me, and have sent me away from you? And they said, We saw plainly that the LORD was with thee; and we said, Let there now be an oath betwixt us, even betwixt us and thee, and let us make a covenant with thee, that thou wilt do us no hurt, as we have not touched thee, and as we have done unto thee nothing but good, and have sent thee away in peace: thou art now the blessed of the LORD. And he made them a feast, and they did eat and drink. And they rose up betimes in the morning, and sware one to another; and Isaac sent them away, and they departed from him in peace.

And it came to pass the same day, that Isaac's servants came, and told him concerning the well which they had digged, and said unto him, We have found water. And he called it Shibah; therefore the name of the city is Beersheba unto this day.

XXI

THE TWIN PEOPLES

A FRAGMENT of family genealogy characteristic of the Elohist is introduced at the end of Chapter xxvi., stating the marriage of Esau at the age of forty. Then follows another ethnic myth illustrative of the relations of Israel and Edom, much more elaborate than that at the end of Chapter xxv., and obviously from a different source. It seems to be mainly the work of the Jehovist, whose peculiar inventive genius is plainly recognizable. What would appear extremely reprehensible in the conduct of individuals, from a moral point of view, loses all moral quality when regarded as a mythological representation of an existing state of things between nations.

Edom, the older nation, had been subjugated by Israel in the time of David, held in subjection until the time of Joram, and reconquered by Amaziah, but finally it broke loose again and shook the yoke from off its neck. It was regarded as of the same origin as Israel, combining the ethnic elements of the South and the North personified in Isaac and Rebekah, but as having been supplanted and outdone in the race of life by the superior qualities of the younger of the twin peoples, with the complicity of divine favor. This condition of things, regarded from the Israelite point of view, actually existed in the time of the writer, and the deception practised in the story may illustrate the moral standard of the time, but it has no other moral significance, when we regard the characters as figuring the relations of nations and of events in a purely mythological sense.

The same view explains the impossibility of revoking the blessing obtained by imposing upon a blind father, though one might naturally expect it to be turned into a curse. It expressed accomplished facts which could not be changed. The "blessings" in rhythmical form are older than the context, and may have been from poetical material out of which the substance of the whole story was extracted. Esau, synonymous with the "shaggy" region of Seir, appears as a hairy man in this story, but there is no reference to the redness of Edom; and the name "Jacob" receives a different explanation from that of the simpler tale of Chapter xxv. As in other cases, the real or supposed meaning of the names of persons and places, together with known characteristics and circumstances, furnished the elements out of which the myth was wrought. No doubt the special affection of Rebekah for Jacob was expressive of a close amity between Syria and Israel and gave it a sentimental bond, while Edom was repelled from any alliance or attachment in that quarter. The reference in the blessing of Jacob to his "brethren," over whom he was to be "lord," is incidental evidence that all these names and relations pertained to lands and peoples and not to persons, for the story gives Jacob no brother except Esau. It was the pre-eminence of Israel over kindred peoples that was expressed, and it was to its power that "the nations" were to bow.

[XXVI 34–XXVII 45]

[And when Esau was forty years old he took to wife Judith the daughter of Beeri the Hittite, and Basemath the daughter of Elon the Hittite; and they were a grief of mind unto Isaac and to Rebekah.]

And it came to pass, that when Isaac was old, and his eyes were dim, so that he could not see, he called Esau his elder son, and said unto him, My son: and he said unto him, Here am I. And he said, Behold now, I am old, I know not the day of my death. Now therefore take, I pray thee, thy weapons, thy quiver and thy bow, and go out to the field, and take me game; and make me savoury food, such as I love, and bring it to me, that I may eat; that my soul may bless thee before I die.

And Rebekah heard when Isaac spake to Esau his son. And Esau went to the field to hunt for game, and to bring it. And Rebekah spake unto Jacob her son, saying, Behold, I heard thy father speak unto Esau thy brother, saying, Bring me game, and make me savoury food, that I may eat, and bless thee before the LORD before my death. Now therefore, my son, obey my voice according to that which I command thee. Go now to the flock, and fetch me from thence two good kids of the goats; and I will make them savoury food for thy father, such as he loveth; and thou shalt bring it to thy father, that he may eat, so that he may bless thee before his death.

And Jacob said to Rebekah his mother, Behold, Esau my brother is a hairy man, and I am a smooth man. My father peradventure will feel me, and I shall seem to him as a deceiver; and I shall bring a curse upon me, and not a blessing. And his mother said unto him, Upon me be thy curse, my son; only obey my voice, and go fetch me them. And he went, and fetched, and brought them to his mother; and his mother made savoury food, such as his father loved. And Rebekah took the goodly garments of Esau her elder son, which were with her in the house, and put them upon Jacob her younger son; and she put the skins of the kids of the goats upon his hands, and upon the smooth of his neck; and she gave the savoury meat and the bread, which she had prepared, into the hand of her son Jacob.

And he came unto his father, and said, My father: and he said, Here am I; who art thou, my son? And Jacob said unto his father, I am Esau thy firstborn; I have done according as thou badest me; arise, I pray thee, sit and eat of my game, that thy soul may bless me. And Isaac said unto his son, How is it that thou hast found it so quickly, my son? And he said, Because the LORD thy God sent me good speed. And Isaac said unto Jacob, Come near, I pray thee, that I may feel thee, my son, whether thou be my very son Esau or not. And Jacob went near unto Isaac his father; and he felt him, and said, The voice is Jacob's voice, but the hands are the hands of Esau.

And he discerned him not, because his hands were hairy, as his brother Esau's hands; so he blessed him. And he said, Art thou my very son Esau? And he said, I am. And he said, Bring it near to me, and I will eat of my son's game, that my soul may bless thee. And he brought it near to him, and he did eat; and he brought him wine, and he drank.

And his father Isaac said unto him, Come near now, and kiss me, my son. And he came near, and kissed him; and he smelled the smell of his garments, and blessed him, and said,

> See, the smell of my son
> Is as the smell of a field which the LORD hath blessed:
> And God give thee of the dew of heaven,
> And of the fatness of the earth,
> And plenty of corn and wine:
> Let peoples serve thee,
> And nations bow down to thee:
> Be lord over thy brethren,
> And let thy mother's sons bow down to thee:
> Cursed be every one that curseth thee,
> And blessed be every one that blesseth thee.

And it came to pass, as soon as Isaac had made an end of blessing Jacob, and Jacob was yet scarce gone out from the presence of Isaac his father, that Esau his brother came in from his hunting. And he also made savoury food, and brought it unto his father; and he said unto his father, Let my father arise, and eat of his son's game, that thy soul may bless me. And Isaac his father said unto him, Who art thou? And he said, I am thy son, thy firstborn, Esau. And Isaac trembled very exceedingly, and said, Who then is he that hath taken game, and brought it me, and I have eaten of all before thou camest, and have blessed him? yea, and he shall be blessed.

When Esau heard the words of his father, he cried with an exceeding great and bitter cry, and said unto his father, Bless me, even me also, O my father. And he said, Thy brother came with guile, and hath taken away thy blessing. And he said, Is not he rightly named Jacob? for he hath supplanted me these two times; he took away my birthright, and, behold, now he hath taken away my blessing. And he said, Hast thou not reserved a blessing for me?

And Isaac answered and said unto Esau, Behold, I have made him thy lord, and all his brethren have I given to him for servants; and with grain and wine have I sustained him; and what then shall I do for thee, my son? And Esau said unto his father, Hast thou but one blessing, my father? bless me, even me also, O my father. And Esau lifted up his voice, and wept. And Isaac his father answered and said unto him,

Behold, of the fatness of the earth shall be thy dwelling,
And of the dew of heaven from above;
And by thy sword shalt thou live, and thou shalt serve thy brother;
And it shall come to pass when thou shalt break loose,
That thou shalt shake his yoke from off thy neck.

And Esau hated Jacob because of the blessing wherewith his father blessed him; and Esau said in his heart, The days of mourning for my father are at hand; then will I slay my brother Jacob. And the words of Esau her elder son were told to Rebekah; and she sent and called Jacob her younger son, and said unto him, Behold, thy brother Esau, as touching thee, doth comfort himself, purposing to kill thee. Now therefore, my son, obey my voice, and arise, flee thou to Laban my brother to Haran; and tarry with him a few days, until thy brother's fury turn away; until thy brother's anger turn away from thee, and he forget that which thou hast done to him; then I will send, and fetch thee from thence. Why should I be bereaved of you both in one day?

XXII

JACOB'S JOURNEY TO SYRIA

THE migration of Jacob to Haran in the land of Syria is represented in the story above cited as due to the anger of Esau and the fears of Rebekah. This story, which is interrupted at verse 45, Chapter xxvii., is resumed at verse 10 of Chapter xxviii., in the familiar division of our Bibles. The break is filled with a passage — in brackets below — from a different source, attaching to the fragment at the end of Chapter xxvi. Esau has been represented as marrying two Hittite wives, to the grief of his father and mother, and now the mother appears as determined that Jacob shall not do likewise, and as sending him with his father's blessing to seek a wife among her kinsmen.

This prosaic passage has the qualities of the Elohist, who never exhibited Jacob and Esau (or Isaac and Ishmael) as alienated. It is said here that Esau, when he saw that his father was not pleased with the daughters of Canaan, and had sent Jacob to Paddan-aram for a wife, tried to make amends by adding to his own domestic circle, as a third wife, his cousin, a daughter of Ishmael. He evidently considered the blood of his father's family just as good as that of his mother's. When the genealogy of Esau is introduced later on in Chapter xxxvi., we shall find that one of his Canaanite wives is said to be a Hittite and one a Hivite, instead of both being daughters of Heth, and that two of the names of his wives are differently given, while the third is transferred from the daughter of Elon the Hittite to the daughter of Ishmael. These inconsistencies are important only as showing once more the character of the material and the difference of source.

The imaginative quality and the religious and ethnical purpose of the Jehovist reappear strongly when the story of Jacob's journey from Beersheba to Haran is resumed, but the writer is evidently transmuting an ancient myth, and the touch of the compiler is also seen in the familiar phrases of the repeated promise of the land to Jacob's posterity. Evidence of the independent origin of the various legends, which pervades the whole Book of Genesis, appears distinctly in this passage. We have seen Abraham in two widely different characters, and when a wife was sought for Isaac a stately caravan was sent, with rich presents, to bring her from a willing kindred. Though Isaac has also been represented as attaining wealth and greatness, his son goes forth alone, to wander through the country and seek favor among his mother's people, afterwards working for years as a common herdsman to win his two wives.

In one legend, already used by the compiler, the consecration and naming of Bethel was attributed to Abraham. Here it is assigned to Jacob in a more mystical way. The "angels" of the dream were those mysterious manifestations of divinity in one or many forms — personified divine influences — of which we have noted other examples. The same symbolical sense of the term appears in the "angels of God ascending and descending upon the Son of Man" in the New Testament. But this mystical picture does not appear to have come from the same account as that which told of Jacob's setting up the stone pillar and making his vow thereon, for in the latter he seems unconscious of the promise of the dream. The statement of the vow is quite prosaic, and evidently intended to assign a divine origin to the requirement of tithes, as in the scene of Abraham and Melchizedek.

[XXVII 46-XXVIII]

[And Rebekah said to Isaac, I am weary of my life because of the daughters of Heth. If Jacob take a wife of the daughters of Heth, such as these, of the daughters of the land, what good shall my life do me?

And Isaac called Jacob, and blessed him, and charged him, and said unto him, Thou shalt not take a wife of the daughters of Canaan. Arise, go to Paddan-aram, to the house of Bethuel thy mother's father; and take thee a wife from thence of the daughters of Laban thy mother's brother. And God Almighty bless thee, and make thee fruitful, and multiply thee, that thou mayest be a company of peoples; and give thee the blessing of Abraham, to thee, and to thy posterity with thee; that thou mayest inherit the land of thy sojournings, which God gave unto Abraham.

And Isaac sent away Jacob; and he went to Paddan-aram unto Laban, son of Bethuel the Syrian, the brother of Rebekah, Jacob's and Esau's mother. Now Esau saw that Isaac had blessed Jacob and sent him away to Paddan-aram, to take him a wife from thence; and that as he blessed him he gave him a charge, saying, Thou shalt not take a wife of the daughters of Canaan; and that Jacob obeyed his father and his mother, and was gone to Paddan-aram: and Esau saw that the daughters of Canaan pleased not Isaac his father; and Esau went unto Ishmael, and took unto the wives which he had Mahalath the daughter of Ishmael, Abraham's son, the sister of Nebaioth, to be his wife.]

And Jacob went out from Beersheba, and went toward Haran. And he lighted upon a certain place, and tarried there all night, because the sun was set; and he took one of the stones of the place and put it under his head, and lay down in that place to sleep. And he dreamed, and behold a ladder set upon the earth, and the top of it reached to heaven; and behold the angels of God ascending and descending on it.

And, behold, the LORD stood before him, and said, I am the LORD the God of Abraham thy father, and the God of Isaac; the land whereon thou liest, to thee will I give it, and to thy posterity; and thy posterity shall be as the dust of the earth, and thou shalt spread abroad to the west, and to the east, and to the north, and to the south; and in thee and in thy offspring shall all the families of the earth be blessed. And, behold, I am with thee, and will keep thee whithersoever thou goest, and will bring thee again into this land; for I will not leave thee until I have done that which I have spoken to thee of.

And Jacob awaked out of his sleep, and he said: Surely the LORD is in this place, and I knew it not; and he was afraid, and said, How dreadful is this place! this is none other but the house of God, and this is the gate of heaven.

And Jacob rose up early in the morning, and took the stone that he had put under his head, and set it up for a pillar, and poured oil upon the top of it. And he called the name of that place Beth-el, but the name of the city was Luz at the first. And Jacob vowed a vow, saying, If God will be with me, and keep me in this way that I go, and will give me bread to eat, and raiment to put on, so that I come again to my father's house in peace, then shall the LORD be my God, and this stone, which I have set up for a pillar, shall be God's house; and of all that thou shalt give me I will surely give the tenth unto thee.

XXIII

JACOB'S DOUBLE MARRIAGE

THE ancient kinship of Israel and Syria was illustrated in the story of Abraham and Nahor, and again in that of the marriage of Isaac and Rebekah. Still greater stress is laid upon it in the more elaborate story of the double marriage of Jacob with the daughters of Laban, and the development therefrom of the several tribes. The myth is in a different tone from the others, and has a deeper and wider ethnic significance. Its Northern, or Ephramite, origin is beyond question, and it prepares the way for defining the relative position of the tribes from that point of view. The mother of the most favored was the beauty of the Syrian family, was the younger, and is to be represented as barren until especially blessed with offspring, a common device of ancient Hebrew story for exhibiting divine preference.

Brilliant eyes were the chief token of beauty to Oriental taste, and the older, less favored, but more prolific wife had dull ("tender") eyes. The coming exaltation of Joseph is made evident in this idyllic tale. In the course of its development, four tribes are to be set lower than the children of Leah, and represented as the offspring of handmaids. The statements, in the account of the marriage, of the giving of the handmaids have the appearance of being interjected by the compiler to prepare the way for later incidents, as they break abruptly into the context. There are also indications of a double source for the main story. The first part speaks only of Rachel as "the daughter" of Laban, and Jacob meets her and falls in love with her at the well, when his superior strength is exhibited in rolling away the stone, which the shepherds could only move when they came together with their flocks. Afterwards we are informed, as if in a different version of the tale, that Laban had two daughters, the younger and more beautiful of whom Jacob loved.

There is an apparent omission of details belonging to varying material in the scanty statement of the bargain in a double form by which Jacob in one form of statement was to receive Rachel as a wife in lieu of "wages" for his service to Laban, and in the other was to serve seven years for the wife in lieu of the customary payment in Oriental contracts of the kind. The imposing of the older and undesired daughter upon the bridegroom by a trick, is intended still further to degrade the origin of the other tribes in comparison with those which sprang from Joseph.

[XXIX 1-30]

Then Jacob went on his journey, and came to the land of the children of the east. And he looked, and behold a well in the field, and, lo, three flocks of sheep lying there by it, for out of that well they watered the flocks; and the stone upon the well's mouth was great. And thither were all the flocks gathered; and they rolled the stone from the well's mouth, and watered the sheep, and put the stone again upon the well's mouth in its place.

And Jacob said unto them, My brethren, whence are ye? And they said, Of Haran are we. And he said unto them, Know ye Laban the son of Nahor? And they said, We know him. And he said unto them, Is it well with him? And they said, It is well; and, behold, Rachel his daughter cometh with the sheep. And he said, Lo, it is yet high day, neither is it time that the cattle should be gathered together; water ye the sheep, and go and feed them. And they said, We cannot, until all the flocks be gathered together, and they roll the stone from the well's mouth; then we water the sheep.

While he yet spake with them, Rachel came with her father's sheep; for she kept them. And it came to pass, when Jacob saw Rachel the daughter of Laban his mother's brother, and the sheep of

Laban his mother's brother, that Jacob went near, and rolled the stone from the well's mouth, and watered the flock of Laban his mother's brother. And Jacob kissed Rachel, and lifted up his voice, and wept. And Jacob told Rachel that he was her father's brother, and that he was Rebekah's son; and she ran and told her father.

And it came to pass, when Laban heard the tidings of Jacob his sister's son, that he ran to meet him, and embraced him, and kissed him, and brought him to his house. And he told Laban all these things. And Laban said to him, Surely thou art my bone and my flesh. And he abode with him the space of a month. And Laban said unto Jacob, Because thou art my brother, shouldest thou therefore serve me for naught? tell me, what shall thy wages be?

And Laban had two daughters; the name of the elder was Leah, and the name of the younger was Rachel. And Leah's eyes were dull; but Rachel was beautiful and well favoured. And Jacob loved Rachel; and he said, I will serve thee seven years for Rachel thy younger daughter. And Laban said, It is better that I give her to thee, than that I should give her to another man; abide with me. And Jacob served seven years for Rachel; and they seemed unto him but a few days, for the love he had to her. And Jacob said unto Laban, Give me my wife, for my days are fulfilled, that I may go in unto her.

And Laban gathered together all the men of the

place, and made a feast. And it came to pass in the evening, that he took Leah his daughter, and brought her to him; and he went in unto her. [And Laban gave Zilpah his handmaid unto his daughter Leah for an handmaid.] And it came to pass in the morning that, behold, it was Leah; and he said to Laban, What is this thou hast done unto me? did not I serve with thee for Rachel? wherefore then hast thou beguiled me? And Laban said, It is not so done in our place, to give the younger before the firstborn. Fulfil the week of this one, and we will give thee the other also for the service which thou shalt serve with me yet seven other years. And Jacob did so, and fulfilled her week; and he gave him Rachel his daughter to wife. [And Laban gave to Rachel his daughter Bilhah his handmaid to be her handmaid.] And he went in also unto Rachel, and he loved also Rachel more than Leah, and served with him yet seven other years.

XXIV

THE BIRTH OF JACOB'S SONS

The account of the birth of Jacob's sons is figurative of the origin of the tribes, as their names and relative standing were known in the writer's time, and regarded from his point of view. The actual origin of the names is unknown, and their etymological significance is uncertain, but the fanciful derivations given in the story come in some cases from mere casual resemblance to familiar words with which they had no real linguistic relation. In the case of Issachar two applications are made of the meaning of the word "hire," one indicating that the name was given because Leah had hired her husband for the night, and the other because she had received her "hire" for giving her handmaid to Jacob. Zebulun is derived from two words similar in form but quite different in meaning, one signifying dowry and the other dwelling. The double derivation of Joseph is from words quite opposite in meaning, "asaf," to take away, and "iasaf," to add. These incongruities

THE BIRTH OF JACOB'S SONS

come not simply from a rough assumption of the meaning of names which have a resemblance to other words, but from the blending of statements and phrases from different sources by the compiler who made up the narrative in its final form.

With regard to the giving of handmaids to the husband by the wife and the accepting of the children of such unions, it may be noted that it was a recognized form of adopting such offspring into the family. Without formality of the kind, children of such parentage were common, but were not recognized as legitimate. Significance is given to the incident of the "love apples," or fruit of the mandrake, by the Oriental belief that they stimulated fecundity. There is in this story of Jacob in Syria no question of the birth of Benjamin, though in the Elohist genealogy at the end of Chapter xxxv. he is enumerated among the sons of Jacob "born to him in Paddan-aram." The Jehovist had a way of his own of accounting for Benjamin. The two brief statements which are put in brackets are foreign to the original material and apparently interpolated by the compiler, the latter perhaps in anticipation of an episode in which Dinah figures. Elsewhere there is no definite reference to a daughter in Jacob's family, as there was no occasion for any in fulfilling the purpose of the ethnical scheme.

[XXIX 31–XXX 24]

And the LORD saw that Leah was hated, and he opened her womb; but Rachel was barren. And Leah conceived, and bare a son, and she called his name Reuben; for she said, Because the LORD hath looked upon my affliction; for now my husband will love me. And she conceived again, and bare a son; and said, Because the LORD hath heard that I am hated, he hath therefore given me this son also: and she called his name Simeon. And she conceived again, and bare a son; and said, Now this time will my husband be joined unto me, because I have borne him three sons: therefore was his name called Levi. And she conceived again, and bare a son, and she said, This time will I praise the LORD: therefore she called his name Judah, and she left bearing.

And when Rachel saw that she bare Jacob no children, Rachel envied her sister; and she said unto Jacob, Give me children, or else I die. [And Jacob's anger was kindled against Rachel; and he said, Am I in God's stead, who hath withheld from thee the fruit of the womb?] And she said, Behold my maid Bilhah, go in unto her, that she may bear upon my knees, and I also may obtain children by her. And she gave him Bilhah her handmaid to wife; and Jacob went in unto her. And Bilhah

THE BIRTH OF JACOB'S SONS

conceived, and bare Jacob a son. And Rachel said, God hath judged me, and hath also heard my voice, and hath given me a son: therefore called she his name Dan. And Bilhah Rachel's handmaid conceived again, and bare Jacob a second son. And Rachel said, With mighty wrestlings have I wrestled with my sister, and have prevailed: and she called his name Naphtali.

When Leah saw that she had left bearing, she took Zilpah her handmaid, and gave her to Jacob to wife. And Zilpah Leah's handmaid bare Jacob a son. And Leah said, Fortunate! and she called his name Gad. And Zilpah Leah's handmaid bare Jacob a second son. And Leah said, Happy am I! for the daughters will call me happy: and she called his name Asher.

And Reuben went in the days of wheat harvest, and found love apples in the field, and brought them unto his mother Leah. Then Rachel said to Leah, Give me, I pray thee, of thy son's love apples. And she said unto her, Is it a small matter that thou hast taken away my husband? and wouldest thou take away my son's love apples also? And Rachel said, Therefore he shall lie with thee to-night for thy son's love apples.

And Jacob came from the field in the evening, and Leah went out to meet him, and said, Thou must come in unto me; for I have surely hired thee with my son's love apples. And he lay with her that night. And God hearkened unto Leah, and she conceived, and bare Jacob a fifth son. And

Leah said, God hath given me my hire, because I gave my handmaid to my husband: and she called his name Issachar. And Leah conceived again, and bare a sixth son to Jacob. And Leah said, God hath endowed me with a good dowry; now will my husband dwell with me, because I have borne him six sons: and she called his name Zebulun. [And afterwards she bare a daughter, and called her name Dinah.]

And God remembered Rachel, and God hearkened to her, and opened her womb. And she conceived, and bare a son; and said, God hath taken away my reproach: and she called his name Joseph, saying, The LORD add to me another son.

XXV

JACOB AND LABAN — ISRAEL AND SYRIA

THE story of the birth of Jacob's sons, from Reuben to Joseph, represents them all as seeing the light during the second seven years of the father's service with Laban; for it is after the birth of Joseph that Jacob proposes to return to his own country, reminding Laban that he has completed the service to which he was bound. This indicates a tradition in the time of the writer that the tribes had their origin in the Mesopotamia region and were closely related to the Syrians, though the latter were earlier possessors of the land of Paddan-aram.

What follows implies that by their superior sagacity and thrift, the Israelites tended to absorb the wealth and power of the country from the Labanites, with the natural result of producing jealousy and quarrel. The picturesque story of the way in which Jacob grew rich at the expense of his uncle and father-in-law by appropriating to himself only the exceptional in the product of the flocks — the striped and spotted among the goats and the black among the sheep — was another illustration of the divine favor that followed the ancestor of the Israelites. The evidence of two widely different forms of this story in the original material is unmistakable, and, as usual, the compiler leaves us this evidence by failing to efface the inconsistencies.

One of these versions shows the same lack of religious tone, and the same disposition to attribute craftiness to Jacob in his dealings, that appeared in the accounts of his gaining advantage over his brother Esau. Laban had proposed that he name his wages for remaining in the service, as affairs had prospered under his hand, and he made the offer of taking only the striped and spotted of the increase of the goats and the black of the lambs, after having separated out all such from the flocks, so that they should not propagate therein. Then he resorted to the trick of the partially peeled rods, which would scarcely prove efficacious in actual practice, though it may serve in a myth.

But when Jacob explains to his wives his reason for leaving their father, there is no suggestion of this. He is the one who has been imposed upon, Laban having changed his wages ten times, sometimes giving him the speckled of the flocks and again the streaked or the grisled, and so on. The mature animals, thus marked, had not been separated from the rest, but were made specially prolific by divine favor to the defeat of all Laban's selfish designs and the enrichment of Jacob. This could hardly have been drawn from the same version of the story as that which precedes, and the transmuting touch of the devout Jehovist is plainly visible, especially in the appearance of God in a dream, reminding of the vow of Bethel, and commanding Jacob to return to the land of his nativity.

The response of Rachel and Leah is not quite so heartless as it seems in our familiar translation. They were "sold" only in the ordinary way of disposing of daughters to husbands, and the father had had the benefit of the price — "devoured our money" does not fairly express it. The subsequent transfer of his substance, it is implied, was the act of God. But when we keep in mind that all this is a mythological representation of the relations of lands and of peoples, family sentiment does not seem really to be involved.

Where material, foreign to that mainly used, can be distinctly separated from the context, it is put in brackets in the passage below. The only fragment that can be identified as from the Elohist document is that at the end. The others are apparently due to the Jehovist narrator incorporating the material of two versions into one, or, possibly, it was the compiler who modified the Jehovist story with material foreign to it. The only thing altogether beyond dispute is the composite character of the account as we have it.

[XXX 25-XXXI 18]

And it came to pass, when Rachel had borne Joseph, that Jacob said unto Laban, Send me away, that I may go unto mine own place, and to my country. Give me my wives and my children for whom I have served thee, and let me go, for thou knowest my service wherewith I have served thee.

And Laban said unto him, If now I have found favour in thine eyes, — I have divined that the LORD hath blessed me for thy sake. And he said, Appoint me thy wages, and I will give it. And he said unto him, Thou knowest how I have served thee, and how thy cattle hath fared with me. For it was little which thou hadst before I came, and it hath increased unto a multitude; and the LORD hath blessed thee whithersoever I turned; and now when shall I provide for mine own house also? And he said, What shall I give thee?

And Jacob said, Thou shalt not give me aught; if thou wilt do this thing for me, I will again feed thy flock and keep it. I will pass through all thy flock to-day, removing from thence every speckled and spotted one, and every black one among the sheep, and the spotted and speckled among the goats; and of such shall be my hire. So shall my righteousness answer for me hereafter, when thou shalt come concerning my hire that is before thee; every one that is not speckled and spotted among the goats, and black among the sheep, if found with me shall be counted stolen. And Laban said, Behold, I would it might be according to thy word.

And he removed that day the he-goats that were striped and spotted, and all the she-goats that were speckled and spotted, every one that had white in it, and all the black ones among the sheep, and gave them into the hand of his sons; and he set three days' journey betwixt himself and Jacob; and Jacob fed the rest of Laban's flocks.

[And Jacob took him rods of fresh poplar, and of the almond and of the plane tree; and peeled white streaks in them, and made the white appear which was in the rods. And he set the rods which he had peeled over against the flocks in the gutters in the watering troughs where the flocks came to drink; and they conceived when they came to drink. And the flocks conceived before the rods, and the flocks brought forth striped, speckled, and spotted.] And Jacob separated the lambs, and set the faces of the flocks toward the striped and all the black in the flock of Laban; and he put his own droves apart, and put them not unto Laban's flock.

[And it came to pass, whensoever the stronger of the flock did conceive, that Jacob laid the rods before the eyes of the flock in the gutters, that they might conceive among the rods; but when the flock were feeble, he put them not in; so the feebler were Laban's, and the stronger Jacob's.] And the man increased exceedingly, and had large flocks, and maidservants and menservants, and camels and asses.

And he heard the words of Laban's sons, saying, Jacob hath taken away all that was our father's; and of that which was our father's hath he gotten all this wealth. And Jacob beheld the countenance of Laban, and, behold, it was not toward him as beforetime. And the LORD said unto Jacob, Return unto the land of thy fathers, and to thy kindred; and I will be with thee.

And Jacob sent and called Rachel and Leah to the field unto his flock, and said unto them, I see your father's countenance, that it is not toward me as beforetime; but the God of my father hath been with me. And ye know that with all my power I have served your father. And your father hath deceived me, and changed my wages ten times; but God suffered him not to hurt me. If he said thus, The speckled shall be thy wages; then all the flock bare speckled: and if he said thus, The striped shall be thy wages; then bare all the flock striped. Thus God hath taken away the cattle of your father, and given them to me.

And it came to pass at the time that the flock conceived, that I lifted up mine eyes, and saw in a dream, and, behold, the he-goats which leaped upon the flock were striped, speckled, and grisled. And the angel of God said unto me in the dream, Jacob! and I said, Here am I. And he said, Lift up now thine eyes, and see, all the he-goats which leap upon the flock are striped, speckled, and grisled; for I have seen all that Laban doeth unto thee. I am the God of Beth-el, where thou anointedst a pillar, where thou vowedst a vow unto me; now arise, get thee out from this land, and return unto the land of thy nativity.

And Rachel and Leah answered and said unto him, Is there yet any portion or inheritance for us in our father's house? Are we not counted of him strangers? for he hath sold us, and hath also quite consumed the price paid for us. For all the riches which God hath taken away from our father, that is ours and our children's; now then, whatsoever God hath said unto thee, do. [Then Jacob rose up, and set his sons and his wives upon the camels; and he carried away all his cattle, and all his substance which he had gathered, the cattle of his getting, which he had gathered in Paddan-aram, for to go to Isaac his father unto the land of Canaan.]

XXVI

THE DIVISION AND TREATY

It is evident that the compiler made another change in his material at verse 19 of Chapter xxxi., at which point the passage given below begins. He had just started Jacob off in a dignified manner with his family on camels, and with his cattle and substance, "to go to Isaac his father unto the land of Canaan," but now we see Jacob in a different guise, sneaking away toward the mountain of Gilead, with stolen "gods" in the possession of his favorite wife, and Laban pursuing after, and very justly upbraiding him for his unworthy manner of taking leave. The quarrel growing out of the theft of the teraphim and the stealing away from the country was a rather primitive device for explaining the ancient division between Israel and Syria, and for leading up to the agreement by which the traditional boundary was fixed, and a friendly alliance established.

Laban appears in the more favorable light throughout this incident, and it is in a spirit of kindly concession and not of claiming his own that he says Jacob's possessions are his. The

THE DIVISION AND TREATY

daughters and the children and the flocks have come from his family and his substance, and are not those of an alien or enemy; and therefore is he ready to enter into the covenant, confirming them to his son-in-law and establishing the limits of their future possessions. The statement of the actual ceremony of treaty-making is confused, and contains elements of two accounts; for in one place Jacob sets up the stone pillar and makes the heap of stones and in another place Laban, and there is a double statement of the eating together as part of the formality.

The relation of names to the forming of this myth of the ancient separation and subsequent alliance of Israel and Syria is worthy of note. The natural boundary was the rocky ridge of Gilead, which was not etymologically the same as Galeed (a stone heap), and the commanding height which formed a military rallying-place had been naturally enough called Mizpah, the "watch-tower." It will be noticed that Laban is represented as giving the Aramaic name and Jacob the Hebrew name to the same spot, at a time when their language must have been the same, assuming this to be a matter of history, and long before the Hebrew forms of speech had been developed through contact with the despised Canaanites and the Phœnicians. The statement as to the names is regarded by scholars as foreign to the context, and it may have been interjected by the compiler.

Another conspicuous place in the same region was Mahanaim, which meant "two camps," the name coming from some event perhaps forgotten in the writer's time, but he attributes it to the meeting there of "God's host." The original term for "angels of God" is the same phrase of which we have spoken as signifying a kind of symbolical manifestation of deity. The ethnical significance of the whole incident is directly revealed in the phrase "Jacob and his brethren," to designate one party to the covenant; for, literally speaking, Jacob had no "brethren"; and something of the prevalent conception of deity appears in the reference to the separate gods of Abraham and Nahor and the common gods (in the plural) of their father. It was long after the writer's day that the Israelites attained a clear conception of God as something more than the special deity of a nation or a people.

[XXXI 19-XXXII 2]

Now Laban was gone to shear his sheep, and Rachel stole the teraphim that were her father's.

And Jacob stole away unawares to Laban the Syrian, in that he told him not that he fled. So he fled with all that he had; and he rose up, and passed over the River, and set his face toward the mountain of Gilead.

And it was told Laban on the third day that Jacob was fled. And he took his brethren with him, and pursued after him seven days' journey; and he overtook him in the mountain of Gilead. And God came to Laban the Syrian in a dream of the night, and said unto him, Take heed to thyself that thou speak not to Jacob either good or bad. And Laban came up with Jacob. Now Jacob had pitched his tent in the mountain, and Laban with his brethren pitched in the mountain of Gilead.

And Laban said to Jacob, What hast thou done, that thou hast stolen away unawares to me, and carried away my daughters as captives of the sword? Wherefore didst thou flee secretly, and steal away from me, and didst not tell me, that I might have sent thee away with mirth and with songs, with tabret and with harp; and hast not suffered me to kiss my sons and my daughters? Now hast thou done foolishly. It is in the power of my hand to do you hurt, but the God of your father spake unto me yesternight, saying, Take heed to thyself that thou speak not to Jacob either good or bad. And now, though thou wouldest needs be gone, because thou sore longedst after thy father's house, yet wherefore hast thou stolen my gods?

And Jacob answered and said to Laban, Because

I was afraid; for I said, Lest thou shouldest take thy daughters from me by force. With whomsoever thou findest thy gods, he shall not live; before our brethren discern thou what is thine with me, and take it to thee. For Jacob knew not that Rachel had stolen them. And Laban went into Jacob's tent, and into Leah's tent, and into the tent of the two maidservants; but he found them not. And he went out of Leah's tent, and entered into Rachel's tent. Now Rachel had taken the teraphim, and put them under the camel's saddle, and sat upon them. And Laban felt about all the tent, but found them not. And she said to her father, Let not my lord be angry that I cannot rise up before thee; for the manner of women is upon me. And he searched, but found not the teraphim.

And Jacob was wroth, and chode with Laban; and Jacob answered and said to Laban, What is my trespass? what is my sin, that thou hast hotly pursued after me? Whereas thou hast felt about all my stuff, what hast thou found of all thy household stuff? Set it here before my brethren and thy brethren, that they may judge betwixt us two. This twenty years have I been with thee; thy ewes and thy she-goats have not cast their young, and the rams of thy flocks have I not eaten. That which was torn of beasts I brought not unto thee, I bare the loss of it; of my hand didst thou require it, whether stolen by day or stolen by night. Thus I was; in the day the drought consumed me, and the frost by night; and my sleep fled from mine eyes. These twenty years have I been in thy house; I served thee fourteen years for thy two daughters, and six years for thy flock; and thou hast changed my wages ten times. Except the God of my father, the God of Abraham, whom Isaac feared, had been with me, surely now hadst thou sent me away empty. God hath seen mine affliction and the labour of my hands, and rebuked thee yesternight.

And Laban answered and said unto Jacob, The daughters are my daughters, and the children are my children, and the flocks are my flocks, and all that thou seest is mine; and what can I do this day unto these my daughters, or unto their children which they have borne? And now come, let us make a covenant, I and thou; and let it be for a witness between me and thee.

And Jacob took a stone, and set it up for a pillar. And Jacob said unto his brethren, Gather stones; and they took stones, and made a heap; and they did eat there by the heap. [And Laban called it Jegar-sahadutha; but Jacob called it Galeed.] And Laban said, This heap is witness between me and thee this day. Therefore was the name of it called Galeed, and Mizpah; for he said, The LORD watch between me and thee, when we are absent one from another. If thou shalt afflict my daughters, and if thou shalt take wives beside my daughters, no man is with us; see, God is witness betwixt me and thee.

And Laban said to Jacob, Behold this heap, and

behold the pillar, which I have set betwixt me and thee. This heap be witness, and the pillar be witness, that I will not pass over this heap to thee, and that thou shalt not pass over this heap and this pillar unto me, for harm. The God of Abraham, and the God of Nahor, the gods of their father, judge betwixt us. And Jacob sware by the God whom his father Isaac feared. And Jacob offered a sacrifice in the mountain, and called his brethren to eat bread; and they did eat bread, and tarried all night in the mountain. And early in the morning Laban rose up, and kissed his sons and his daughters, and blessed them; and Laban departed, and returned unto his place. And Jacob went on his way, and the angels of God met him. And Jacob said when he saw them, This is God's host: and he called the name of that place Mahanaim.

XXVII

JACOB AND ESAU — ISRAEL AND EDOM

IF we were dealing with accounts of actual personal conduct, it would seem like a foolish proceeding for Jacob, on his way from Syria to the northern part of Canaan, to send word to Esau in the distant land of Seir, and then to exhibit such dread of meeting him. But there is little doubt that the story of a personal meeting is a mythical embodiment of traditions of an encounter with Edomites in the early migration from the North and a truce by which peaceable relations were established. What appears both foolish and cowardly as personal behavior represents actual conditions and relations in the conduct of tribes, of which one was warlike and had fixed possessions, and the other was peaceable and nomadic.

It was consistent with the theocratic spirit, which began with the early Hebrew writers, to acknowledge the superior warlike qualities of Edom, and to represent Israel in a submissive, not to say cowardly, attitude, and as escaping hostility by crafty evasion and the making of presents. While it seems craven in personal conduct, it is expressive of the policy solemnly inculcated by those who taught reliance upon Jehovah in all national troubles.

The story of Jacob's encounter with Esau, near the northern boundary of Israel's future possessions east of the Jordan, is broken into two parts by the interpolation of one of those mystical episodes of which the Jehovist narrator was so fond, and both parts show the usual evidence of diversity of material which was imperfectly blended by the compiler. In the first part suggestions from the meaning of Mahanaim appear in the relation of Jacob's devices for escaping what he assumes will be the anger of a wronged brother; but they appear in two different forms. First we are told that Jacob divided his caravan into two companies, so that if Esau attacked one the other might escape. Then, after the prayer for deliverance, the twofold division appears again in the sending forward of flocks and herds as a present to appease Esau, separated by a safe distance from the family.

The episode of the wrestling by the ford is a curious example of the evolution of mythical meanings from the names of places and persons and from familiar facts. The name of the brook

Jabbok resembled a word meaning "to wrestle." Peniel or Penuel meant, or appeared to mean, "the face of God." The word "Israel," which had been the designation of that branch of the Hebrew race which took possession of Canaan from time immemorial, while Jacob was a poetical and oratorical equivalent for the same people, was of doubtful derivation, but was assumed to mean God's warrior or champion. There is no reference elsewhere to the custom of not eating the sinew from the hollow of the thigh, but it is here assumed to be a custom. Out of these elements was formed the story whose main purpose seems to be to account for the name "Israel," and to exalt Jacob not only as one who contended for God, but contended with him and prevailed. The explanatory statement that "the children of Israel eat not the sinew of the hip" seems to drop one suddenly from the realm of myth to the compiler's prosaic time.

After this interruption the story of the meeting with Esau is resumed in a form little corresponding to the preparation, and having no relation to the probabilities of actual personal experience. The family is ranged in three divisions in the reverse order of the rank of the tribes, regarded from the Josephite writer's point of view, because there is assumed to be danger at the front in meeting "my lord" Esau. But the chief of Edom proves gracious to his humble kindred, and reluctant to accept the proffered gift. There is a marvellous condensation of ethnical meaning and expression of Israelite traits in Jacob's simulation of joy at meeting his powerful brother, and in his device for separation from him under pretence of following him to the land of Seir, while avoiding the proffered escort.

Doubtless this all belongs to the folk-lore of a time when Israel was suspicious and fearful of the power of the warlike Edom, and had either established relations of peace or was anxious to do so, and it was associated in the story with the migration from Mesopotamia to Canaan, after the division of territory with Syria, when there might well have been fears of encountering Edomites from the South. Jacob's pretended purpose of following his brother home was of course immediately forgotten, and he established his people's right of possession on the east of the Jordan by building a house and calling the place Succoth. The proof of this was the existence of such a place, the name meaning virtually "cattle-sheds."

[XXXII 3-XXXIII 17]

And Jacob sent messengers before him to Esau his brother unto the land of Seir, the field of Edom. And he commanded them, saying, Thus shall ye say unto my lord Esau; Thus saith thy servant Jacob, I have sojourned with Laban, and stayed until now; and I have oxen, and asses and flocks, and menservants and maidservants; and I have sent to tell my lord, that I may find grace in thy sight.

And the messengers returned to Jacob, saying, We came to thy brother Esau, and moreover he cometh to meet thee, and four hundred men with him. Then Jacob was greatly afraid and was distressed; and he divided the people that were with him, and the flocks, and the herds, and the camels, into two companies; and he said, If Esau come to the one company, and smite it, then the company which is left shall escape.

And Jacob said, O God of my father Abraham, and God of my father Isaac, O LORD, which saidst unto me, Return unto thy country, and to thy kindred, and I will do thee good: I am not worthy of the least of all the mercies, and of all the truth, which thou hast shewed unto thy servant; for with my staff I passed over this Jordan; and now I am become two companies. Deliver me, I pray thee, from the hand of my brother, from the hand of Esau; for I fear him, lest he come and smite me, the mother with the children. And thou saidst, I will surely do thee good, and make thy posterity as the sand of the sea, which cannot be numbered for multitude.

And he lodged there that night; and took of that which he had with him a present for Esau his brother; two hundred she-goats and twenty he-goats, two hundred ewes and twenty rams, thirty milch camels and their colts, forty kine and ten bulls, twenty she-asses and ten foals. And he delivered them into the hand of his servants, every drove by itself; and said unto his servants, Pass over before me, and put a space betwixt drove and drove. And he commanded the foremost, saying, When Esau my brother meeteth thee, and asketh thee, saying, Whose art thou? and whither goest thou? and whose are these before thee? then thou shalt say, They are thy servant Jacob's; it is a present sent unto my lord Esau, and, behold, he also is behind us. And he commanded also the second, and the third, and all that followed the droves, saying, On this manner shall ye speak unto Esau, when ye find him; and ye shall say, Moreover, behold, thy servant Jacob is behind us. For he said, I will appease him with the present that goeth before me, and afterward I will see his face; peradventure he will accept me. So the present passed over before him; and he himself lodged that night in the company.

And he rose up that night, and took his two wives, and his two handmaids, and his eleven children, and passed over the ford of Jabbok. And he took them, and sent them over the stream, and sent over that he had.

And Jacob was left alone; and there wrestled a man with him until the breaking of the day. And when he saw that he prevailed not against him, he touched the hollow of his thigh; and the hollow of Jacob's thigh was strained, as he wrestled with him. And he said, Let me go, for the day breaketh. And he said, I will not let thee go, except thou bless me. And he said unto him, What is thy name? And he said, Jacob. And he said, Thy name shall be called no more Jacob, but Israel; for thou hast striven with God and with men, and hast prevailed. And Jacob asked him, and said, Tell me, I pray thee, thy name. And he said, Wherefore is it that thou dost ask after my name? And he blessed him there. And Jacob called the name of the place Peniel; for, said he, I have seen God face to face, and my life is preserved. And the sun rose upon him as he passed over Penuel, and he went halting upon his thigh. [Therefore the children of Israel eat not the sinew of the hip which is upon the hollow of the thigh, unto this day; because he touched the hollow of Jacob's thigh in the sinew of the hip.]

And Jacob lifted up his eyes, and looked, and, behold, Esau came, and with him four hundred men. And he divided the children unto Leah, and unto Rachel, and unto the two handmaids. And he put the handmaids and their children foremost, and Leah and her children after, and Rachel and Joseph hindermost. And he himself passed over before them, and bowed himself to the ground seven times, until he came near to his brother.

And Esau ran to meet him, and embraced him, and fell on his neck, and kissed him; and they wept. And he lifted up his eyes, and saw the women and the children; and said, Who are these with thee? And he said, The children which God hath graciously given thy servant. Then the handmaids came near, they and their children, and they bowed themselves. And Leah also and her children came near, and bowed themselves; and after came Joseph near and Rachel, and they bowed themselves.

And he said, What meanest thou by all this company which I met? And he said, To find grace in the sight of my lord. And Esau said, I have enough; my brother, let that thou hast be thine. And Jacob said, Nay, I pray thee, if now I have found grace in thy sight, then receive my present at my hand; forasmuch as I have seen thy face, as one seeth the face of God, and thou wast pleased with me. Take, I pray thee, my gift that is brought to thee; because God hath dealt graciously with me, and because I have enough. And he urged him, and he took it.

And he said, Let us take our journey, and let us go, and I will go before thee. And he said unto him, My lord knoweth that the children are tender, and that the flocks and herds with me have their young; and if they overdrive them one day, all the flocks will die. Let my lord, I pray thee, pass over before his servant; and I will lead on slowly, according to the pace of the cattle that is before me and according to the pace of the children, until I come unto my lord unto Seir. And Esau said, Let me now leave with thee some of the folk that are with me. And he said, What needeth it? let me find grace in the sight of my lord. So Esau returned that day on his way unto Seir. And Jacob journeyed to Succoth, and built him an house, and made booths for his cattle; therefore the name of the place is called Succoth.

XXVIII

AT SHECHEM — THE STORY OF DINAH

There is no account in the compiler's narrative of Jacob crossing the Jordan and making his way over the country, but we are suddenly told that he came in peace to Shechem and encamped before the city. This statement (in italics below) is from the Elohist. He bought ground and built an altar, which symbolized in the Jehovist story, from which this was derived, the taking possession of the country.

The statements of the arrival at Shechem served to introduce the curious tale of Dinah, the sole daughter of Jacob, whose birth in Paddan-aram has been barely mentioned. The purely ethnic and mythic character of this tale is revealed throughout in the most artless manner. Shechem is used indifferently as a place and as a person. In the outrage upon Dinah he is said to have "wrought folly in Israel" at a time when "Israel" is supposed to be a personal name for Jacob, according to one account just conferred, and according to another not yet conferred, by divine designation.

Again, the connecting passage of the compiler represents Jacob as having just arrived from Paddan-aram, all his children, including Dinah, having been born within the last dozen years, and being too "tender" on the journey to admit of the caravan keeping pace with Esau's march. And yet here his sons appear not merely as grown-up men, but as promising on certain conditions to give their daughters as wives to the men of the land, while Simeon and Levi are such formidable warriors as to inflict indiscriminate slaughter upon the males of Shechem, to spoil the city, take the women and children captive, and appropriate the wealth of the place.

It needs no argument to prove that all this has no relation to literal facts. The story seems to have been made up from two versions sufficiently wrought together to destroy their separate identity, but not sufficiently to efface the signs of difference. The account of the proposal of marriage between Shechem and Dinah and of a general intermarriage was originally independent of that of the violation of the maiden, and a bewildering mixture of purposes confuses the passage as it stands.

In many ways in these old writings was the injunction conveyed that there should be no marrying with the native people of the land, who should the rather be exterminated, as with the sword of Simeon and Levi. In some elements of this story there appears evidence of a desire to degrade the children of Leah, and one possible purpose of the incident of the slaughter at Shechem was to displace from popular memory, at a time when it was the sole repository of passing records, the actual occurrence of outrage and bloodshed in the days of the "judges," when Gideon's son Abimelech, an Ephraimite, tried to make himself king.

Some critics have undertaken so to divide the story of Dinah as to exhibit the elements of the two versions, of which one represents the maiden as being abused by Shechem (to the vindictive wrath of her brothers), and the other relates a friendly effort to secure her marriage with the Son of Hamor, and a general intermarriage between the two peoples, which was met by a treacherous device of the sons of Jacob to destroy the Shechemites and get possession of their wealth. These two are supposed to have been combined by the compiler by the simple process of patching together passages from each in such a manner as to produce the appearance of a single narrative. As a matter of curious interest, the story is so divided below as to exhibit these diverse elements in alternative paragraphs.

According to Lenormant, that which begins with Dinah's going out to visit the daughters of the land, and gives an account of innocent efforts to bring about a marriage, ending with the treacherous violence of Simeon and Levi, and Jacob's rebuke of their conduct, was contained in the Elohist document, while that which told of the defiling of Dinah and the attempted reparation by marriage, and speaks of the revenge of the "Sons of Jacob" without mentioning names, was from the Jehovist. It will be observed that neither designation for the deity appears at all, and there is no religious quality in the story. There certainly appears to have been two of these tales, the main purpose of which was to serve as a warning against intermarriage with the Canaanites and to beget an aversion to it. The compiler, instead of adopting one in preference to the other, undertook to make one out of the two. To make clearer the distinction between what are regarded as different sources, the paragraphs credited to the less prominent are put in brackets.

[XXXIII 18–XXXIV]

And Jacob came in peace to the city of Shechem, which is in the land of Canaan, when he came from Paddan-aram; and encamped before the city. And he bought the parcel of ground, where he had spread his tent, at the hand of the children of Hamor, Shechem's father, for an hundred pieces of money. And he erected there an altar, and called it El-elohe-Israel.

And Dinah the daughter of Leah, which she bare unto Jacob, went out to see the daughters of the land. And Shechem the son of Hamor the Hivite, the prince of the land, saw her;
[And he took her, and lay with her, and humbled her. And his soul clave unto Dinah the daughter of Jacob, and he loved the damsel, and spake kindly unto the damsel.]
And Shechem spake unto his father Hamor, saying, Get me this damsel to wife.
[Now Jacob heard that he had defiled Dinah his daughter, and his sons were with his cattle in the field; and Jacob held his peace until they came.]
And Hamor the father of Shechem went out unto Jacob to commune with him.
[And the sons of Jacob came in from the field when they heard it; and the men were grieved, and they were very wroth, because he had wrought folly in Israel in lying with Jacob's daughter; which thing ought not to be done.]

AT SHECHEM — THE STORY OF DINAH

And Hamor communed with them, saying, The soul of my son Shechem longeth for your daughter; I pray you give her unto him to wife. And make ye marriages with us; give your daughters unto us, and take our daughters unto you. And ye shall dwell with us; and the land shall be before you; dwell and trade ye therein, and get you possessions therein.

[And Shechem said unto her father and unto her brethren, Let me find grace in your eyes, and what ye shall say unto me I will give. Ask me never so much dowry and gift, and I will give according as ye shall say unto me; but give me the damsel to wife. And the sons of Jacob answered Shechem and Hamor his father with guile, and spake, because he had defiled Dinah their sister, and said unto them, We cannot do this thing, to give our sister to one that is uncircumcised; for that were a reproach unto us:]

Only on this condition will we consent unto you: if ye will be as we be, that every male of you be circumcised; then will we give our daughters unto you, and we will take your daughters to us, and we will dwell with you, and we will become one people. But if ye will not hearken unto us, to be circumcised; then will we take our daughter, and we will be gone. And their words pleased Hamor, and Shechem Hamor's son.

[And the young man deferred not to do the thing, because he had delight in Jacob's daughter; and he was honoured above all the house of his father.]

And Hamor and Shechem his son came unto the gate of their city, and communed with the men of their city, saying, These men are peaceable with us; therefore let them dwell in the land, and trade therein; for, behold, the land is large enough for them; let us take their daughters to us for wives, and let us give them our daughters. Only on this condition will the men consent unto us to dwell with us, to become one people, if every male among us be circumcised, as they are circumcised. Shall not their cattle and their substance and all their beasts be ours? only let us consent unto them, and they will dwell with us. And unto Hamor and unto Shechem his son hearkened all that went out of the gate of his city; and every male was circumcised, all that went out of the gate of his city. And it came to pass on the third day, when they were sore, that two of the sons of Jacob, Simeon and Levi, Dinah's brethren, took each man his sword, and came upon the city unawares, and slew all the males.

[And they slew Hamor and Shechem his son with the edge of the sword, and took Dinah out of Shechem's house, and went forth. The sons of Jacob came upon the slain, and spoiled the city, because they had defiled their sister.]

They took their flocks and their herds and their asses, and that which was in the city, and that which was in the field;

[And all their wealth, and all their little ones and their wives, took they captive and spoiled, even all that was in the house.]

And Jacob said to Simeon and Levi, Ye have troubled me, to make me odious among the inhabitants of the land, among the Canaanites and the Perizzites; and, I being few in number, they will gather themselves together against me and smite me; and I shall be destroyed, I and my house.

[And they said, Should he deal with our sister as with an harlot?]

XXIX

BETHEL AND AFTER

Not only is there another complete change in the character and tone of the narrative at the beginning of Chapter xxxv. but that chapter is made up of three passages quite distinct from each other, and containing plain evidences of a difference in their sources, though there are conspicuous indications in all three that the Elohist document was again drawn upon. In fact, the genealogical passage at the end seems to be wholly from that source.

First we have an account of a re-consecration of Bethel, in which there is a reference to that version of Jacob's journey to Paddan-aram which represented him as fleeing from the anger of Esau. There is no indication of his previous dwelling-place, but he is told to "go up to Bethel and dwell there," and to "make there an altar to God." This is one of the tales which symbolized the possession of that sacred place, the discarding of idolatry and its emblems, which included rings worn as amulets in the ears, and devotion to the worship of "El" on the ancient height of Luz. It indicates the previous existence among the people of polytheism, whose tokens, brought from Syria, by stealth, were to be buried by the terebinth of Shechem. This passage seems to be fragmentary, and the tradition of the death of Rebekah's nurse at a place where there was a tree known as "the oak of weeping" is brought in with a strange irrelevancy. There is no intimation elsewhere that the nurse of Jacob's mother had attended him in his varied wanderings, and one would have supposed her dead long before this time.

The passage which immediately follows this contains yet another account of the consecration of Bethel, and of the giving of that name to the place, though it has been already attributed once to Abraham, and twice to Jacob. The incident is said to have occurred when Jacob "came from Paddan-aram," and then and there also his name was changed to Israel, though we have had quite another account of that in the occurrence by the ford of Jabbok. The form of consecration by setting up a pillar and pouring out a libation and anointing with oil is generally characteristic of the Elohist, where the Jehovist and the compiler writing in his own person speak of the building of an altar and making sacrifices.

An ethnic fragment is brought in here relating to the birth of Benjamin, on a journey from the North to the South. The derivation of the name of that tribe has been variously explained, and while "yamin" meant "right," the warriors of the tribe were distinguished for a skilful use of the left hand. They were called Beni-yamin, sons of the right or skilled hand, apparently because they were ambidextrous, or skilled with both hands, — right-handed as it were, on both sides. Hence the etymological paradox of their being called sons of the right hand because they used their weapons with the left hand, which made them specially effective as slingers and javelin-throwers. The interpretation of "right" as favorable or fortunate, with reference to omens, seems to be without support in Hebrew ideas. The Samaritans derived the name from "yamim," "days," indicating the son of old age, but the chronology of these narratives is greatly mixed and not significant of much.

There were two traditions of Rachel's tomb, one of which placed it at Bethlehem and the other north of Jerusalem (1 Sam. x. 2). It is easy to imagine, but impossible to prove, that the compiler interpolated here the irrelevant statement of Reuben's offence, deriving it from the poem which we shall find later on, commonly known as Jacob's "blessing" of his sons.

The bit of genealogy at the end of the chapter is noteworthy for including Benjamin among the twelve sons of Jacob "born to him in Paddan-aram," for making Hebron the dwelling-place of Isaac, and for representing Esau and Jacob as still in personal relations and joining in the burial of their father. These are unmistakable characteristics of the Elohist and quite inconsistent with the Jehovist narratives, which placed Isaac at Beersheba, set enmity between Esau and Jacob, and long ago sent the former to the wilderness of Mount Seir as a hunter and warrior. These differences are of supreme interest as proof of the diversity of material and of the purely ethnical significance of these so-called records.

The confused chronology is important only in the same view. For instance, Isaac was sixty years old when Jacob was born, and he dies at one hundred and eighty, making the son one hundred and twenty; but Jacob was forty when he went to Paddan-aram, and he remained there twenty years. This would give an interval of sixty years between his return and his father's death. But Joseph was born in Paddan-aram and must have been living these sixty years, while we are yet to see him sent to Egypt at the age of seventeen and becoming Pharaoh's prime minister at thirty.

[XXXV]

And God said unto Jacob, Arise, go up to Beth-el, and dwell there; and make there an altar unto God, who appeared unto thee when thou fleddest from the face of Esau thy brother.

Then Jacob said unto his household, and to all that were with him, Put away the strange gods that are among you, and purify yourselves, and change your garments; and let us arise, and go up to Beth-el; and I will make there an altar unto God, who answered me in the day of my distress, and was with me in the way which I went. And they gave unto Jacob all the strange gods which were in their hand, and the rings which were in their ears; and Jacob hid them under the terebinth which was by Shechem.

And they journeyed; and terror of God was upon the cities that were round about them, and they did not pursue after the sons of Jacob. So Jacob came to Luz, which is in the land of Canaan (the same is Beth-el), he and all the people that were with him. And he built there an altar, and called the place El-beth-el, because there God was revealed unto him when he fled from the face of his brother.

And Deborah Rebekah's nurse died, and she was buried below Beth-el under the oak; and the name of it was called Allon-bacuth (*the oak of weeping*).

[And God appeared unto Jacob again, when he came from Paddan-aram, and blessed him. And God said unto him, Thy name is Jacob; thy name shall not be called any more Jacob, but Israel shall be thy name: and he called his name Israel. And God said unto him, I am God Almighty (*El Shaddai*); be fruitful and multiply; a nation and a union of nations shall be of thee, and kings shall come out of thy loins; and the land which I gave unto Abraham and Isaac, to thee I will give it, and to thy race after thee will I give the land. And God went up from him in the place where he spake with him. And Jacob set up a pillar in the place where he spake with him, a pillar of stone; and he poured out a drink offering thereon, and poured oil thereon. And Jacob called the name of the place where God spake with him, Beth-el.]

And they journeyed from Beth-el; and there was still some way to come to Ephrath; and Rachel travailed, and she had hard labour. And it came to pass, when she was in hard labour, that the midwife said unto her, Fear not; for now thou shalt have another son. And it came to pass, as her soul was in departing (for she died), that she called his name Ben-oni; but his father called him Benjamin. And Rachel died, and was buried in the way to Ephrath (the same is Beth-lehem). And Jacob set up a pillar upon her grave; the same is the Pillar of Rachel's grave unto this day. And Israel journeyed, and spread his tent beyond the tower of

Eder. [And it came to pass, while Israel dwelt in that land, that Reuben went and lay with Bilhah his father's concubine; and Israel heard of it.]

[Now the sons of Jacob were twelve: the sons of Leah; Reuben, Jacob's firstborn, and Simeon, and Levi, and Judah, and Issachar, and Zebulun: the sons of Rachel; Joseph and Benjamin: and the sons of Bilhah, Rachel's handmaid; Dan and Naphtali: and the sons of Zilpah, Leah's handmaid; Gad and Asher: these are the sons of Jacob, which were born to him in Paddan-aram. And Jacob came unto Isaac his father to Mamre, to Kiriath-arba (the same is Hebron), where Abraham and Isaac sojourned. And the days of Isaac were an hundred and fourscore years. And Isaac gave up the ghost, and died, and was gathered unto his people, old and full of days; and Esau and Jacob his sons buried him.]

XXX

EDOMITE ETHNOGRAPHY

IMMEDIATELY after giving us a view of Esau joining with his brother Jacob in the burial of their father at Hebron, the compiler introduces an ethnographical account of Edom, obviously made up of diverse fragments. The repetitions and inconsistencies indicate that additions and corrections had been crudely made. The general purpose was to indicate that the Edomites, whose domain was substantially that of Arabia Petræa, were of mixed blood and widely alienated from the pure strain of the descendants of Abraham, which was preserved only in Israel. They were mingled not only with the Canaanites and Ishmaelites, but with the Horites, who were the indigenous people of the Mount Seir region.

The first paragraph, as the text is printed below, is clearly from the Elohist document, and only presents the three main branches of the Edomite stock as offspring of Esau's wives, two of whom were from separate Canaanite tribes and the other was a daughter of Ishmael. This writer represents the separation of Esau and Jacob as occurring after the birth of the former's five sons, and an undefined number of daughters, and as being a peaceable arrangement due to the increase of their possessions. The incongruity of this picture with the Jehovist's account of the enmity of the two brothers, and especially with the story of their encounter when Jacob was returning from Paddan-aram and Esau came with an army from Mount Seir, where he had been established long before, is sufficiently manifest.

The second paragraph, in the division below, is quite independent of this, but corresponds in the names of the wives and sons of Esau. It carries the genealogy just far enough to account for the traditional twelve tribes of Edom, and the roving and predatory Amalekites, who are set aside as the offspring of a concubine.

In the next paragraph we have a repetition of the names as of the chiefs of tribes, but this is followed by a personification of the aborigines of the Mount Seir wilderness as the sons of Seir the Horite. But the names are in part the same as those which figure among the descendants of Esau, and the relationships are confused. Anah, for instance, who has been called a son of Zibeon, the Hivite, is made both the brother and the son of

Zibeon, who is a Horite. In fact, the names in both cases are mostly those of places, though some of them have a meaning denoting animals. Zibeon means a hyena, and Anah a wild ass, for instance.

These writings are not far from contemporaneous with the Book of Job, and it is interesting to note the correspondence between Eliphaz as the father of Teman and Eliphaz the Temanite, and to find Uz among the descendants of Seir. Uz also appears in the ethnography of Genesis x. among the descendants of Shem.

The account of the "kings that reigned in the land of Edom before there reigned any king over the children of Israel" is curious as naïvely revealing the fact that the author was writing in the time of the kings in Israel, if indeed he ever had any idea of concealing that fact. Some have thought to identify Jobab in this line of kings with Job, but that is fanciful. There is a brief repetition or variation of a list of Edomite chiefs, in which Timna and Oholibamah figure, though these have previously appeared as a concubine and a wife respectively of Esau. These were really the names of places like Uz and Teman.

The sentences in brackets at the end are a

broken fragment used by the compiler to form a rude connecting link between two utterly unrelated passages in his work. The last sentence appears to have been introductory to a genealogy of Jacob, which does not follow.

[XXXVI]

Now these are the generations of Esau (the same is Edom). Esau took his wives of the daughters of Canaan; Adah the daughter of Elon the Hittite, and Oholibamah the daughter of Anah, the daughter of Zibeon the Hivite; and Basemath Ishmael's daughter, sister of Nebaioth. And Adah bare to Esau Eliphaz; and Basemath bare Reuel; and Oholibamah bare Jeush, and Jalam, and Korah: these are the sons of Esau, which were born unto him in the land of Canaan. And Esau took his wives, and his sons, and his daughters, and all the souls of his house, and his cattle, and all his beasts, and all his possessions, which he had gathered in the land of Canaan; and went into a land away from his brother Jacob. For their substance was too great for them to dwell together; and the land of their sojournings could not bear them because of their cattle. And Esau dwelt in mount Seir. Esau is Edom.

And these are the generations of Esau the father of the Edomites in mount Seir: these are the names

EDOMITE ETHNOGRAPHY 243

of Esau's sons; Eliphaz the son of Adah the wife of Esau, Reuel the son of Basemath the wife of Esau. And the sons of Eliphaz were Teman, Omar, Zepho, and Gatam, and Kenaz. And Tamna was concubine to Eliphaz Esau's son; and she bare to Eliphaz Amalek: these are the sons of Adah Esau's wife. And these are the sons of Reuel; Nahath, and Zerah, Shammah, and Mizzah: these were the sons of Basemath Esau's wife. And these were the sons of Oholibamah the daughter of Anah, the daughter of Zibeon, Esau's wife; and she bare to Esau Jeush, and Jalam, and Korah.

These are the chiefs of the sons of Esau: the sons of Eliphaz the firstborn of Esau; chief Teman, chief Omar, chief Zepho, chief Kenaz, chief Korah, chief Gatam, chief Amalek: these are the chiefs that came of Eliphaz in the land of Edom; these are the sons of Adah. And these are the sons of Reuel Esau's son; chief Nahath, chief Zerah, chief Shammah, chief Mizzah: these are the chiefs that came of Reuel in the land of Edom; these are the sons of Basemath Esau's wife. And these are the sons of Oholibamah Esau's wife; chief Jeush, chief Jalam, chief Korah: these are the chiefs that came of Oholibamah the daughter of Anah, Esau's wife. These are the sons of Esau, and these are their chiefs. The same is Edom.

These are the sons of Seir the Horite, the inhabitants of the land; Lotan and Shobal and Zibeon and Anah, and Dishon and Ezer and Dishan: these are the chiefs that came of the Horites, the children of Seir in the land of Edom. And the children of Lotan were Hori and Hemam; and Lotan's sister was Timna. And these are the children of Shobal; Alvan and Manahath and Ebal, Shepho and Onam. And these are the children of Zibeon; Aiah and Anah: [this is Anah who found the hot springs in the wilderness, as he fed the asses of Zibeon his father]. And these are the children of Anah; Dishon and Oholibamah the daughter of Anah. And these are the children of Dishon; Hemdan and Eshban and Ithran and Cheran. These are the children of Ezer; Bilhan and Zaavan and Akan. These are the children of Dishan; Uz and Aran. These are the chiefs that came of the Horites; chief Lotan, chief Shobal, chief Zibeon, chief Anah, chief Dishon, chief Ezer, chief Dishan: these are the chiefs that came of the Horites, according to their chiefs in the land of Seir.

And these are the kings that reigned in the land of Edom, before there reigned any king over the children of Israel. And Bela the son of Beor reigned in Edom; and the name of his city was Dinhabah. And Bela died, and Jobab the son of Zerah of Bozrah reigned in his stead. And Jobab died, and Husham of the land of the Temanites reigned in his stead. And Husham died, and Hadad the son of Bedad, who smote Midian in the field of Moab, reigned in his stead; and the name of his city was Avith. And Hadad died, and Samlah of Masrekah reigned in his stead. And

Samlah died, and Shaul of Rehoboth by the River reigned in his stead. And Shaul died, and Baal-hanan the son of Achbor reigned in his stead. And Baal-hanan the son of Achbor died, and Hadar reigned in his stead; and the name of his city was Pau; and his wife's name was Mehetabel, the daughter of Matred, the daughter of Me-zahab.

And these are the names of the chiefs that came of Esau, according to their families, after their places, by their names; chief Timnah, chief Alvah, chief Jetheth; chief Oholibamah, chief Elah, chief Pinon; chief Kenaz, chief Teman, chief Mibzar; chief Magdiel, chief Iram : these be the chiefs of Edom, according to their habitations in the land of their possession.

[This is Esau the father of the Edomites, and Jacob dwelt in the land of his father's sojournings, in the land of Canaan. These are the generations of Jacob.]

XXXI

JOSEPH AND HIS BRETHREN

If the original author of the story of Joseph and his brethren was familiar with the Abraham, Isaac, and Jacob legends, he took no pains to be consistent with them. As it now stands, it has no congruity with what precedes in the "record," and it furnishes many indications of the manner in which that record was composed.

It assumes, in the application of the dream of the sun and moon and eleven stars, that Joseph's mother was still living. It makes no reference to Leah, but speaks of Bilhah and Zilpah as the father's "wives" and the mothers of Joseph's brethren. One reason given for the hatred of his brethren was jealousy on account of the father's special love of the "son of his old age," and yet, in the account of the birth of the children in Paddan-aram, it appeared that there could not be a difference of more than six or seven years between the oldest and the youngest. Joseph is said to be seventeen years old, but according to the chronology of the genealogical narrator he must have been sixty when Isaac died. If we follow this story and take seventeen as his age when he was sent into Egypt, thirty when Pharaoh put him in charge of great affairs there, and under forty, as it must have been, when Jacob told Pharaoh that the sum of his own "few and evil days" was a hundred and thirty years, then must Jacob have been at least ninety years old when Joseph was born, six years before he left Paddan-aram, and something like seventy-five when he went there. Such inconsistencies dispel all ideas of personal history in these accounts, but are unimportant when they are regarded in their true light as ethnic myths.

There are distinct evidences of the blending of two different tales in the account of Joseph's going to Egypt. The two explanations of the motives of his brothers' hatred, — the father's favoritism, and the self-exaltation of the dreams, — were from different sources. Among the unrealities of the narrative may be mentioned the supposition that dwellers in the vale of Hebron would be feeding their flocks in Shechem, especially after the episode of slaughter there, — of which this writer perhaps knew nothing, — and wandering thence to Dothan, an unidentified place on the caravan route from Damascus to Egypt, and that a lad of seventeen would be sent over that range of hill country occupied by Canaanite tribes to inquire after their welfare.

It is especially in the account of the betrayal of the younger brother, his rescue from death, and the abduction to Egypt, that indications of the blending of two stories are clear. According to one, Reuben rescues the lad by the suggestion that he be put into one of the empty water cisterns which were placed below the level of the ground in those grazing regions. This was consented to, perhaps, with the idea that he would perish there, for the peculiar horror of death by shedding the blood did not attach to perishing by other means. But passing Midianites drew the boy out, carried him to Egypt, and sold him into slavery.

According to the other story he was saved by Judah's suggestion, that instead of killing him they sell him to a caravan of Ishmaelites which happened to pass that way. Details of the stories were omitted to make them fit together, and at the end of this preliminary chapter we are told that the "Midianites sold him into Egypt unto Potiphar," while at the beginning of the chapter in which the narrative is resumed, "Potiphar bought him of the hand of the Ishmaelites." Casual signs of the two stories also appear further on. For instance, Joseph told Pharaoh's chief butler in the prison that he was "stolen away out of the land of the Hebrews" (by the Midianites?), and when he finally revealed himself to his brothers, he told them not to be grieved "that ye sold me hither" (to the Ishmaelites?).

Another of the evidences of mythical origin may be noted in this reference to caravans of Ishmaelites and Midianites passing through the country to trade with Egypt. Jacob's family thus far appears to consist of a dozen children, and when they finally went down to Goshen, some twenty years later, "all the souls of the house of Jacob" were "three score and ten." But the Ishmaelites had been represented as the descendants of his father's half brother, and the Midianites as the progeny of another and much younger half brother. For such near relatives, they had grown numerous and unfriendly at an amazing rate, but in myths and fables, however significant of truths in their own way, historical probability is not to be looked for. The great fact embodied in this story is the vast superiority in the mind of its original author of the character and destiny of the Josephite tribes over the rest of Israel. Its further use was to prepare the way for accounting for the greater fact that the Israelites did at a remote time wander into Egypt and fall into a state of bondage.

In the text below an attempt is made to separate the elements which belong to the two different versions of the story by inclosing in brackets the statements drawn from the one that represents the envy of the brothers as due to the father's favoritism, and Judah as accomplishing Joseph's rescue by the device of selling him to the Ishmaelites. The parts derived from the other version appear by omitting these bracketed statements, and they attribute the hatred for Joseph to his dreams of greatness, and the rescue to Reuben's interposition and the casting of the youth into the "pit," from which he was lifted out and carried away by Midianites. The division is that of Lenormant, who credited the story in which Reuben and the Midianites figure to the Elohist, and that in which Judah and the Ishmaelites appear to the Jehovist. There is little but conjecture to sustain that view, and if it is well founded, it is pretty certain that the material was not original with those writers, though the opening statement of the chapter, which sets out to give the "generations" of Jacob, and is interrupted with the Joseph story, is distinctly of the Elohist. The unquestionable thing is that the compiler of Genesis imperfectly blended into one two stories which were not consistent in their details. It will be interesting to note for future reference that in the elements from one version of the story the father of Joseph is called Jacob, while in those from the other he is called Israel.

[XXXVII]

And Jacob dwelt in the land of his father's sojournings, in the land of Canaan. These are the generations of Jacob.

Joseph, being seventeen years old, was feeding the flock with his brethren; [and he was a lad with the sons of Bilhah, and with the sons of Zilpah, his father's wives:] and Joseph brought the evil report of them unto their father. [Now Israel loved Joseph more than all his children, because he was the son of his old age; and he made him a coat of many colours. And his brethren saw that their father loved him more than all his brethren; and they hated him, and could not speak peaceably unto him.]

And Joseph dreamed a dream, and he told it to his brethren; and they hated him yet the more. And he said unto them, Hear, I pray you, this dream which I have dreamed: for, behold, we were binding sheaves in the field, and, lo, my sheaf arose, and also stood upright; and, behold, your sheaves came round about, and made obeisance to my sheaf. And his brethren said unto him, Shalt thou indeed reign over us? or shalt thou indeed have dominion over us? And they hated him yet the more for his dreams, and for his words. And he dreamed yet another dream, and told it to his brethren, and said, Behold, I have dreamed yet a dream; and, behold, the sun and the moon and eleven stars made obeisance to me. And he told it to his father, and to his brethren; and his father rebuked him, and said unto him, What is this dream that thou hast dreamed? Shall I and thy mother and thy brethren indeed come to bow down ourselves to thee to the earth? And his brethren envied him; but his father kept the saying in his mind.

[And his brethren went to feed their father's flock in Shechem. And Israel said unto Joseph, Do not thy brethren feed the flock in Shechem? come, and I will send thee unto them. And he said to him, Here am I. And he said to him, Go now, see whether it be well with thy brethren, and well with the flock; and bring me word again. So he sent him out of the vale of Hebron, and he came to Shechem. And a certain man found him, and, behold, he was wandering in the field: and the man asked him, saying, What seekest thou? And he said, I seek my brethren; tell me, I pray thee, where they are feeding the flock. And the man said, They are departed hence; for I heard them say, Let us go to Dothan. And Joseph went after his brethren, and found them in Dothan.]

And they saw him afar off, and before he came near unto them, they conspired against him to slay him. And they said one to another, Behold, this dreamer cometh. Come now therefore, and let us slay him, and cast him into one of the pits, and we will say, An evil beast hath devoured him; and we shall see what will become of his dreams. And Reuben heard it, and delivered him out of their hand; and said, Let us not take his life. And Reuben said unto them, Shed no blood; cast him into this pit that is in the wilderness, but lay no hand upon him: that he might deliver him out of their hand, to restore him to his father.

[And it came to pass, when Joseph was come unto his brethren, that they stript Joseph of his coat, the coat of many colours that was on him.]

And they took him, and cast him into the pit; and the pit was empty, there was no water in it.

[And they sat down to eat bread; and they lifted up their eyes and looked, and, behold, a travelling company of Ishmaelites came from Gilead, with their camels bearing spicery and balm and myrrh, going to carry it down to Egypt. And Judah said unto his brethren, What profit is it if we slay our brother and conceal his blood? Come, and let us sell him to the Ishmaelites, and let not our hand be upon him; for he is our brother, our flesh. And his brethren hearkened unto him.]

And there passed by Midianites, merchantmen; and they drew and lifted up Joseph out of the pit, [and sold Joseph to the Ishmaelites for twenty pieces of silver]. And they brought Joseph into Egypt. And Reuben returned unto the pit; and, behold, Joseph was not in the pit; and he rent his clothes. And he returned unto his brethren, and said, The child is not; and I, whither shall I go?

[And they took Joseph's coat, and killed a he-goat, and dipped the coat in the blood; and they sent the coat of many colours, and they brought it to their father; and said, This have we found; know now whether it be thy son's coat or not. And he knew it, and said, It is my son's coat; an evil beast hath devoured him; Joseph is without doubt torn in pieces.]

And Jacob rent his garments, and put sackcloth upon his loins, and mourned for his son many days. And all his sons and all his daughters rose up to comfort him; but he refused to be comforted; and he said, For I will go down to Sheol to my son mourning. And his father wept for him. And the Midianites sold him into Egypt unto Potiphar, an officer of Pharaoh's, the captain of the guard.

XXXII

JUDAH AND HIS FAMILY

PERHAPS it is not strange that the Judean compiler of the Book of Genesis should have retained the story of the exaltation of Joseph at the expense of his brethren. When he wrote, the proud Kingdom of Ephraim had been humiliated and destroyed, and its memories had become a common heritage of the race. Hope of a reunion of the tribes and the establishment of a glorious and enduring Kingdom of all Israel was then cherished. He could afford to be magnanimous, and besides, the story was a fascinating one, and it was an essential part of that great epic of the bondage and deliverance of the people, which formed the basis of their history, their law, and their religion. The compiler could hardly dispense with it, and he was not capable of replacing it. Fortunately he retained it very much as he found it in the collection of Ephraimite productions.

But it does seem strange that between the preliminary story of Joseph's dreams of greatness and the jealousy and treachery of his brethren, and that of the realization of the dreams in power and glory in Egypt, with the humiliation and dependence of the rest of the family, he should have introduced that picture of the degradation of Judah, containing a slightly veiled satire upon the founder of the Judean dynasty, which stands apart from all connection with the context as Genesis xxxviii. Doubtless he did not appreciate the moral turpitude attributed to Judah, and the ignominy attached to his offspring; but he could hardly have missed the general meaning and purpose of the story, which must have originated at a time of harsh feeling between the two kingdoms.

We have seen in the equally independent epopee of Simeon and Levi avenging their sister's wrong at Shechem, that these sons of Jacob appear as mature men with daughters to give in marriage, though we come to the story with fresh impressions of their tender childhood. In the family tale of Paddan-aram, Judah could scarcely have been three years older than Joseph, and we have just seen him attending his father's flocks and joining in the conspiracy to sell the younger brother into Egypt at the age of seventeen. Here we come upon him in quite a different aspect, and with a family history of his own extending over a period of many years. The compiler introduced the story with the familiar "and it came to pass at that time," though it had no relation in time or place with what precedes.

It is difficult to discern any very clear ethnic significance in this episode of Judah and Tamar, though some critics assume that Er and Onan were sub-tribes of mixed Judean and Canaanite blood which had died out. The whole appears much more like a satire upon Judah and the house of David. It begins with a union of the putative ancestor of the kingdom with the despised Canaanite, which appears to have been illegitimate, and not even a marriage, though David himself had taken more than one Canaanite wife. The offence of the first son is not named, but that of the second was disobedience of the "law" which required him to marry the widow and raise up an heir to the oldest son of the family. Failing that, he would himself become the head of the family, and he refused, and the Lord slew him. Judah then tried himself to evade the obligation of the law and get rid of Tamar, who circumvented the design by her own wiles. The part she played was that

s

of one of the female attendants of the impure worship of Astarte (Ashtoreth), which served further to degrade Judah by complicity in the cult most abominable in the eyes of the Puritans of Israel. The prostitution itself was not subject to the penalty of burning, or to any other penalty, unless in the case of Tamar it might be regarded as equivalent to adultery; but she was declared to be "more righteous" than the man who had failed to give her to his younger son as the widow of the elder. That, indeed, was Judah's offence, and so far as the story has an ethical purpose, it was intended to enforce that obligation of keeping the family inheritance in the line of the oldest son. It may be that there was a disposition among the people to evade it, and that the story of the fate of Onan and the humiliation of Judah gave an example of the consequences.

The satire upon the family of David, which is involved in the story, seems palpable when it is closely studied. Even the name of Hirah the Adullamite is suggestive of Hiram the Tyrian, friend of David and Solomon, and of the refuge of David when he was an outlaw. David had married more than one Canaanitess, the most notorious case being that of Bath-Sheba, the sometime wife of the Hittite officer, a name synonymous with Bath-Shua (daughter of Shua). Bath-Shua is given as the "wife" of Judah in the genealogy of the Book of Chronicles.

The first offspring of David and Bath-Sheba died in consequence of divine anger, as does the firstborn of Judah and Bath-Shua. The letters of the name "Er" in Hebrew, spelled backward, mean "bad." The substitution of a single letter in the Hebrew changes Onan to Amnon, the son of David who was destroyed on account of sexual sin. The identity of the name of the outraged sister and the wronged wife of Judah's sons is noticeable, while a close analogy to Amnon's iniquity is transferred to Judah himself, while he is seeking to evade the obligation to give his third son to the widow of the first and second. One letter inserted in the name of that third son in the Hebrew transforms it to Solomon, the son of David and Bath-Sheba, who became the King of Judah against whom Jeroboam rebelled. There may be an additional thrust in the enigmatical remark that "he (Judah) was at Chezib when she (Tamar) bare him" (Shelah), for though Chezib may have been the name of a place, it was also a noun meaning falsehood, and was used in that sense by the prophet Micah.

No offspring is given to Shelah in the story, but the descendants of Judah are made to spring from the iniquitous intercourse with Tamar, and the ancestor of David is Perez, the "breach" or "breaker through," who superseded his twin brother at birth, as Solomon superseded an elder brother in the succession to the throne, which finally led to the Ephraimite revolt. If the relation to history of this episode in the life of Judah, which breaks so abruptly into the narrative of Joseph's going into Egypt to appear as a model of chastity and integrity, is mere coincidence, it makes it only the more remarkable.

If it were to be regarded as a matter of actual personal history, it would be repulsive from a moral point of view, but, while it furnishes a picture of moral conditions at the time of its production, its chief interest is in its mythical or symbolical meanings. It also affords another striking illustration of the varied character and purpose of the productions which were wrought together in the marvellous composition of this Book of Genesis. It furnishes one of the many proofs which that book contains within itself of a complete lack of historical quality, in the literal sense, and of an abundance and variety of mythological quality.

[XXXVIII[1]]

And it came to pass at that time, that Judah went down from his brethren, and turned in to a certain Adullamite, whose name was Hirah. And Judah saw there a daughter of a certain Canaanite whose name was Shua; and he took her, and went in unto her. And she conceived, and bare a son; and he called his name Er. And she conceived again, and bare a son; and she called his name Onan. And she yet again bare a son, and called his name Shelah; and he was at Chezib, when she bare him.

And Judah took a wife for Er his firstborn, and her name was Tamar. And Er, Judah's firstborn, was wicked in the sight of the LORD; and the LORD slew him. And Judah said unto Onan, Go in unto thy brother's wife, and perform the duty of an husband's brother unto her, and raise up offspring to thy brother. And Onan knew that the offspring should not be his; and it came to pass, when he went in unto his brother's wife, that he avoided propagating offspring to his brother. And the thing which he did was evil in the sight of the LORD; and he slew him also.

Then said Judah to Tamar his daughter in law, Remain a widow in thy father's house, till Shelah my son be grown up: for he said, Lest he also die, like

---

[1] The explanation of this chapter as a satire on the family of David was first elaborated by Dr. Aaron Bernstein, author of "Ursprung der Sage von Abraham, Isaak und Jakob."

his brethren. And Tamar went and dwelt in her father's house. And in process of time Shua's daughter, the wife of Judah, died; and Judah was comforted, and went up unto his sheepshearers to Timnah, he and his friend Hirah the Adullamite. And it was told Tamar, saying, Behold, thy father in law goeth up to Timnah to shear his sheep. And she put off from her the garments of her widowhood, and covered herself with her veil, and wrapped herself, and sat in the gate of Enaim, which is by the way to Timnah; for she saw that Shelah was grown up, and she was not given unto him to wife.

When Judah saw her, he thought her to be an harlot; for she had covered her face. And he turned unto her by the way, and said, Go to, I pray thee, let me come in unto thee: for he knew not that she was his daughter in law. And she said, What wilt thou give me, that thou mayest come in unto me? And he said, I will send thee a kid of the goats from the flock. And she said, Wilt thou give me a pledge, till thou send it? And he said, What pledge shall I give thee? And she said, Thy signet and thy cord, and thy staff that is in thine hand. And he gave them to her, and came in unto her, and she conceived by him. And she arose, and went away, and put off her veil from her, and put on the garments of her widowhood.

And Judah sent the kid of the goats by the hand of his friend the Adullamite, to receive the pledge from the woman's hand; but he found her not. Then he asked the men of her place, saying, Where is the harlot, that was at Enaim by the way side? And they said, There hath been no harlot here. And he returned to Judah, and said, I have not found her; and also the men of the place said, There hath been no harlot here. And Judah said, Let her take it to her, lest we be put to shame; behold, I sent this kid, and thou hast not found her.

And it came to pass about three months after, that it was told Judah, saying, Tamar thy daughter in law hath played the harlot; and moreover, behold, she is with child by harlotry. And Judah said, Bring her forth, and let her be burnt. When she was brought forth, she sent to her father in law, saying, By the man, whose these are, am I with child: and she said, Discern, I pray thee, whose are these, the signet, and the cords, and the staff. And Judah acknowledged them, and said, She is more righteous than I; forasmuch as I gave her not to Shelah my son. And he knew her again no more.

And it came to pass in the time of her travail, that, behold, twins were in her womb. And it came to pass, when she travailed, that one put out a hand; and the midwife took and bound upon his hand a scarlet thread, saying, This came out first. And it came to pass, as he drew back his hand, that, behold, his brother came out; and she said, Wherefore hast thou made a breach for thyself? therefore his name was called Perez. And afterward came out his brother, that had the scarlet thread upon his hand; and his name was called Zerah.

XXXIII

JOSEPH A SLAVE AND IN PRISON

The account of Joseph's life in Egypt before he was brought to the notice of Pharaoh contains distinct traces of the blending of two different stories of which we have seen evidences already. According to the opening statement he was bought from the Ishmaelites by Potiphar, chief of Pharaoh's palace guard, and the original language implies that this person was a eunuch. He is identified in the episode of the chief "butler" and the chief "baker"— more properly the chief cup bearer and chief purveyor of bread — and also in the relation of this episode to the king, with the "keeper of the prison," as from his office he might well be.

This could hardly have been the same man as Joseph's "master the Egyptian," whose wife afforded such a serious test of his personal virtue. This "Egyptian" was evidently a man of substance to whose confidence the "Hebrew servant" so commended himself that he was put in charge of "all that he had in the house and in the field."

Neither this, nor the tempting wife, is suggestive of the "captain of the guard." Moreover, are we not told that Joseph's angry master "put him into prison," and that he gained favor in the sight of the "keeper of the prison" and had all the prisoners put in his charge, and does it not presently appear that it was the "captain of the guard" himself who was keeper of the prison? Surely the Egyptian master, whose favor Joseph had first won, and then lost through the wiles of the wife, was not suddenly transformed into the keeper of the prison to have his favor regained.

Apparently the story which represented Joseph as having been sold by his brethren to the Ishmaelites, also represented him as being bought by the "captain of the guard," who had charge of the prison, and as rising in the favor of that officer and having the care of the prisoners committed to him; while the other story, which represented Joseph as having been "stolen away" by the Midianites, told of his having been sold to a rich Egyptian who had him thrown into prison on account of the incident of the wife's intrigue. The name of the man is not mentioned in what we have of this version of the story, and the wife was doubtless not that of Potiphar the eunuch.

Probably both stories led up to the dreams which were to be the means of bringing Joseph to the attention of Pharaoh, a common device in Oriental tales, and traces of the difference disappear except where Joseph speaks of himself as having been "stolen away out of the land of the Hebrews" and "put into a dungeon." This can hardly be from the version in which he was said to have been sold to the Ishmaelites and bought by the officer in charge of the prison, whose chief deputy he became. In connection with this phrase, "land of the Hebrews," and that used by the Egyptian's wife, "the Hebrew servant," it is to be observed that the Israelites were not called "Hebrews," and Canaan could not have been designated as the "land of the Hebrews" until sometime after the establishment of the kingdom. The locution is that of the time of the writer.

As we have had occasion to say so often, these inconsistencies are unimportant when we consider the genuine mythological character of the writings, but they are extremely interesting as evidences of the manner of their production.

[XXXIX–XL]

[And Joseph was brought down to Egypt; and Potiphar, an officer of Pharaoh's, the captain of the guard, an Egyptian, bought him of the hand of the Ishmaelites, which had brought him down thither.]

And the LORD was with Joseph, and he was a prosperous man; and he was in the house of his master the Egyptian. And his master saw that the LORD was with him, and that the LORD made all that he did to prosper in his hand. And Joseph found grace in his sight, and he ministered unto him; and he made him overseer over his house, and all that he had he put into his hand. And it came to pass from the time that he made him overseer in his house, and over all that he had, that the LORD blessed the Egyptian's house for Joseph's sake; and the blessing of the LORD was upon all that he had, in the house and in the field. And he left all that he had in Joseph's hand; and he knew not aught that was with him, save the bread which he did eat.

And Joseph was comely, and well favoured. And it came to pass after these things, that his master's wife cast her eyes upon Joseph; and she said, Lie with me. But he refused, and said unto his master's wife, Behold, my master knoweth not what is with me in the house, and he hath put all that he hath into my hand; there is none greater in this house than I; neither hath he kept back any thing from me but thee, because thou art his wife; how then can I do this great wickedness, and sin against God? And it came to pass, as she spake to Joseph day by day, that he hearkened not unto her, to lie by her, or to be with her. And it came to pass about this time, that he went into the house to do his work; and there was none of the men of the house there within. And she caught him by his garment, saying, Lie with me: and he left his garment in her hand, and fled, and got him out.

And it came to pass, when she saw that he had left his garment in her hand, and was fled forth, that she called unto the men of her house, and spake unto them, saying, See, he hath brought in an Hebrew unto us to mock us; he came in unto me to lie with me, and I cried with a loud voice; and it came to pass, when he heard that I lifted up my voice and cried, that he left his garment by me, and fled, and got him out. And she laid up his garment by her, until his master came home. And she spake unto him according to these words, saying, The Hebrew servant, which thou hast brought unto us, came in unto me to mock me; and it came to pass, as I lifted up my voice and cried, that he left his garment by me, and fled out. And it came to pass, when his master heard the words of his wife, which she spake unto him, saying, After this manner did thy servant to me; that his wrath was kindled.

And Joseph's master took him, and put him into the prison, the place where the king's prisoners were bound; and he was there in the prison. But the LORD was with Joseph, and shewed kindness unto him, and gave him favour in the sight of the keeper of the prison. And the keeper of the prison committed to Joseph's hand all the prisoners that were in the prison; and whatsoever they did there, he was the doer of it. The keeper of the prison looked not to any thing that was under his hand, because the LORD was with him; and that which he did, the LORD made it to prosper.

And it came to pass after these things, that the cup bearer of the king of Egypt and his purveyor of bread offended their lord the king of Egypt. And Pharaoh was wroth against his two officers, against the chief of the cup bearers, and against the chief of the purveyors of bread. And he put them in ward in the house of the captain of the guard, into the prison, [*the place where Joseph was bound*]. And the captain of the guard charged Joseph with them, and he ministered unto them; and they continued a season in ward.

And they dreamed a dream both of them, each man his dream, in one night, each man according to the interpretation of his dream, the cup bearer and the purveyor of bread of the king of Egypt, who were bound in the prison. And Joseph came in unto them in the morning, and saw them, and, behold, they were sad. And he asked Pharaoh's officers [*that were with him in ward in his master's house*], saying, Wherefore look ye so sadly to-day? And they said unto him, We have dreamed a dream, and there is none that can interpret it. And Joseph said unto them, Do not interpretations belong to God? tell it me, I pray you.

And the chief cup bearer told his dream to Joseph, and said to him, In my dream, behold, a vine was before me; and in the vine were three branches; and it was as though it budded, and its blossoms shot forth; and the clusters thereof brought forth ripe grapes; and Pharaoh's cup was in my hand; and I took the grapes, and pressed them into Pharaoh's cup, and I gave the cup into Pharaoh's hand. And Joseph said unto him, This is the interpretation of it: the three branches are three days; within yet three days shall Pharaoh lift up thine head, and restore thee unto thine office; and thou shalt give Pharaoh's cup into his hand, after the former manner when thou wast his cup bearer. But have me in thy remembrance when it shall be well with thee, and shew kindness, I pray thee, unto me, and make mention of me unto Pharaoh, and bring me out of this house; for indeed I was stolen away out of the land of the Hebrews: [*and here also have I done nothing that they should put me into the dungeon.*]

When the chief purveyor of bread saw that the interpretation was good, he said unto Joseph, I also was in my dream, and, behold, three baskets of white bread were on my head; and in the uppermost basket there was of all manner of baked food for Pharaoh; and the birds did eat them out of the basket upon my head. And Joseph answered and said, This is the interpretation thereof: the three baskets are three days; within yet three days shall Pharaoh lift up thy head from off thee, and shall hang thee on a tree; and the birds shall eat thy flesh from off thee. And it came to pass the third day, which was Pharaoh's birthday, that he made a feast unto all his servants; and he lifted up the head of the chief cup bearer and the head of the chief purveyor of bread among his servants. And he restored the chief cup bearer unto his office again, and he gave the cup into Pharaoh's hand; but he hanged the chief purveyor of bread, as Joseph had interpreted to them. Yet did not the chief cup bearer remember Joseph, but forgot him.

XXXIV

JOSEPH'S ELEVATION TO POWER

There is hardly room for doubt that the original story of Joseph was written in the Northern Kingdom of Israel in the time of Jeroboam, its first king. There is no indication that the name Joseph was applied until after that time, as a general designation for the people of the nation made up chiefly of the tribes of Ephraim and Manasseh, with outlying territory known by names assumed to have been originally those of other tribes. The etymology that derived Joseph from a word meaning separation, or taking away, may have had reference to the division of the kingdom. It is a plausible surmise that Jeroboam himself was the originator of the story, if not the inventor of the name attributed to the ancestor of his people.

It will be remembered that Jeroboam had headed a revolt against Solomon and fled "unto Shishak king of Egypt." It may be inferred that he stood high in the favor of that ruler from the fact that a few years after he returned and set up his throne at Shechem as king of the revolted tribes, Shishak gave him substantial support by invading the Kingdom of Judah and laying Jerusalem under contribution. Jeroboam, who was clearly the ablest Israelite of his time, had all the knowledge of Egypt and of its lore necessary for framing the incidents of the Joseph story, and he had the motive for exalting the prototype of his nation at the expense of the rest of Israel, and exhibiting a kindly spirit toward Pharaoh and his realm, — ever the objects of hatred to Judean writers. It was even a matter of pride to represent Ephraim and Manasseh as half Egyptian in blood, though that had been corruption in the story of Ishmael, and in most of the legends intermarriage with peoples not akin to the seed of Abraham was degradation. The man who set up golden calves as symbols of Jehovah at Bethel and Dan could even take the mother of his people from the priesthood of Heliopolis.

The story of Joseph's elevation from slavery and imprisonment to power in the land of Egypt is contained in the forty-first chapter of Genesis, in the traditional division of that book. It contains no element of probability as matter of historical fact, and is supported by no record of such an extraordinary event as seven successive years of marvellous plenty, succeeded by seven years of absolute dearth in the Nile region and all the neighboring lands, and as the exaltation of a Hebrew slave to control of all the affairs of the great Kingdom of Egypt in the height of its power.

The material of Pharaoh's dreams and their fulfilment, and of Joseph's fabulous exaltation, is such stuff as myths are made of, and the evident purpose of the whole story is the glorification of Jeroboam's kingdom. To this the account of Joseph's treatment by his brothers, his being sold into slavery and thrown into prison, and being ever attended by divine care, was preliminary. There is little trace of the variant of the main story in Chapter xli., though Joseph is referred to by the chief cup bearer as "servant to the captain of the guard" in the prison, and is afterwards said to have been brought "hastily out of the dungeon." The original story, it is to be remembered, had passed through the hands of at least two writers before the permanent form was reached, and had assumed two varying versions, one of which was adopted as the basis of a compilation and modified with material from the other as it suited the compiler's notions of completeness. What appear to be interjected sentences are put in brackets below.

[XLI]

And it came to pass at the end of two full years, that Pharaoh dreamed; and, behold, he stood by the river. And, behold, there came up out of the river seven kine, well favoured and fatfleshed; and they fed in the reedgrass. And, behold, seven other kine came up after them out of the river, ill favoured and leanfleshed, and stood by the other kine upon the brink of the river. And the ill favoured and leanfleshed kine did eat up the seven well favoured and fat kine. So Pharaoh awoke.

And he slept and dreamed a second time; and, behold, seven ears of corn came up upon one stalk, rank and good. And, behold, seven ears, thin and blasted with the east wind, sprung up after them. And the thin ears swallowed up the seven rank and full ears. And Pharaoh awoke, and, behold, it was a dream.

And it came to pass in the morning that his spirit was troubled; and he sent and called for all the diviners of Egypt and all the wise men thereof, and Pharaoh told them his dream; but there was none that could interpret them unto Pharaoh. Then spake the chief cup bearer unto Pharaoh, saying, I do remember my faults this day. Pharaoh was wroth with his servants, and put me in ward in the house of the captain of the guard, me and the chief purveyor of bread, and we dreamed a dream in one night, I and he; we dreamed each man according to the interpretation of his dream. And there was with us there a young man, an Hebrew, servant to the captain of the guard; and we told him, and he interpreted to us our dreams, to each man according to his dream he did interpret. And it came to pass, as he interpreted to us, so it was; me he restored unto mine office, and him he hanged.

Then Pharaoh sent and called Joseph, [and they brought him hastily out of the dungeon:] and he shaved himself, and changed his raiment, and came in unto Pharaoh. And Pharaoh said unto Joseph, I have dreamed a dream, and there is none that can interpret it; and I have heard say of thee, that when thou hearest a dream thou canst interpret it. And Joseph answered Pharaoh, saying, It is not in me; God shall give Pharaoh an answer of peace.

And Pharaoh spake unto Joseph, In my dream, behold, I stood upon the brink of the river; and, behold, there came up out of the river seven kine, fatfleshed and well favoured, and they fed in the reedgrass; and, behold, seven other kine came up after them poor and very ill favoured and leanfleshed, such as I never saw in all the land of Egypt for badness, and the lean and ill favoured kine did eat up the first seven fat kine; and when they had eaten them up, it could not be known that they had eaten them; but they were still ill favoured, as at the beginning. So I awoke. And I saw in my dream, and, behold, seven ears came up upon one stalk, full and good; and, behold, seven ears, withered, thin, and blasted with the east wind, sprung up after them; and the thin ears swallowed up the seven good ears; and I told it unto the diviners, but there was none that could declare it to me.

And Joseph said unto Pharaoh, The dream of Pharaoh is one; what God is about to do he hath declared unto Pharaoh. The seven good kine are seven years; and the seven good ears are seven years; the dream is one. And the seven lean and ill favoured kine that came up after them are seven years, and also the seven empty ears blasted with the east wind; they shall be seven years of famine. That is the thing which I spake unto Pharaoh; what God is about to do he hath shewed unto Pharaoh. Behold, there come seven years of great plenty throughout all the land of Egypt; and there shall arise after them seven years of famine; and all the plenty shall be forgotten in the land of Egypt; and the famine shall consume the land; and the plenty shall not be known in the land by reason of that famine which followeth, for it shall be very grievous. And for that the dream was doubled unto Pharaoh twice, it is because the thing is established by God, and God will shortly bring it to pass. Now therefore let Pharaoh look out a man discreet and wise, and set him over the land of Egypt. Let Pharaoh do this, and let him appoint overseers over the land, and take up the fifth part of the land of Egypt in the seven plenteous years. And let them gather all the food of these good years that come, and lay up grain under the hand of Pharaoh for food in the cities, and let them keep it. And the food shall be for a store to the land against the seven years of famine, which shall be in the land of Egypt; that the land perish not through the famine. And the thing was good in the eyes of Pharaoh, and in the eyes of all his servants.

And Pharaoh said unto his servants, Can we find such a one as this, a man in whom the spirit of God is? And Pharaoh said unto Joseph, Forasmuch as God hath shewed thee all this, there is none so discreet and wise as thou, thou shalt be over my house, and according unto thy word shall all my people be ruled; only in the throne will I be greater than thou. And Pharaoh said unto Joseph, See, I have set thee over all the land of Egypt. And Pharaoh took off his signet ring from his hand, and put it upon Joseph's hand, and arrayed him in vestures of fine linen, and put a gold chain about his neck; and he made him to ride in the second chariot which he had; and they cried before him, Bow the knee: and he set him over all the land of Egypt. And Pharaoh said unto Joseph, I am Pharaoh, and without thee shall no man lift up his hand or his foot in all the land of Egypt.

And Pharaoh called Joseph's name Zaphenath-paneah; and he gave him to wife Asenath the daughter of Poti-phera priest of On. And Joseph went out over the land of Egypt. And Joseph was thirty years old when he stood before Pharaoh king of Egypt. And Joseph went out from the presence of Pharaoh, and went throughout all the land of Egypt. And in the seven plenteous years the earth brought forth by handfuls. And he gathered up all the food of the seven years which were in the land of Egypt, and laid up the food in the cities; the food of the field, which was round about every city, laid he up in the same. [And Joseph laid up grain as the sand of the sea, very much, until he left numbering; for it was without number.]

And unto Joseph were born two sons before the year of famine came, which Asenath the daughter of Poti-phera priest of On bare unto him. [And Joseph called the name of the firstborn Manasseh: For, said he, God hath made me forget all my toil, and all my father's house. And the name of the second called he Ephraim: For God hath made me fruitful in the land of my affliction.]

And the seven years of plenty, that was in the land of Egypt, came to an end. And the seven years of famine began to come, according as Joseph had said, and there was famine in all lands; but in all the land of Egypt there was bread. And when all the land of Egypt was famished, the people cried to Pharaoh for bread, and Pharaoh said unto all the Egyptians, Go unto Joseph; what he saith to you, do. And the famine was over all the face of the earth; and Joseph opened all the storehouses, and sold unto the Egyptians; and the famine was sore in the land of Egypt. And all countries came into Egypt to Joseph for to buy grain; because the famine was sore in all the earth.

XXXV

JOSEPH'S BROTHERS SEEK RELIEF IN EGYPT

The artless simplicity of primitive mythism appears throughout the narrative, which tells of Joseph's ten brothers seeking relief from famine in Egypt, while he was "lord of the land." Where Jacob then dwelt, "in the land of Canaan," does not appear, but our last view of him was when he sent his favorite son from "the vale of Hebron" to his brethren feeding their flocks in Shechem and wandering to Dothan; and later we shall find him coming from somewhere to Beersheba. But wherever the patriarch and his family might now be, it must be many days' journey from the storehouses of Egypt. But the ten sons, each with an ass and a sack, make their way in time of famine to Joseph, who is personally selling supplies to all comers. It had never occurred to him in his nine years of prosperity and power to inquire after the family, and his extraordinary advancement had never reached their ears, though communication now seems so easy.

Apparently the brothers had no food on their way down, and on the return the contents of the nine sacks, borne on their humble beasts of burden,—for Simeon was left behind,—must have sufficed for the grain which was to relieve the famine of their "houses," the "provision for the way," and the "provender" for the animals. It would also appear that only one of the sacks was opened at the "lodging place," for it was after they reached home that each man's money was found in his sack, that of only one having been previously discovered. No fairy tale could show a more charming disregard of probabilities, or even possibilities, than this simple narrative. It may seem rather far-fetched to assume that Simeon was the name used for the brother left as a hostage, because of the tradition of a tribe of Simeon which had disappeared near the borders of Egypt; but such slight suggestions were prolific of the incidents of these old legends.

Here Reuben appears as reminding the other brothers of their fault, when they find themselves in trouble, and as afterwards assuring the aged father of Benjamin's safety, in case he is taken to Egypt in fulfilment of the pledge to "the lord of the land," though Judah becomes the surety when the second trip is actually made. In this is an evident trace of the two versions of the story as they first appear in Chapter xxxvii.

The most striking quality in this passage, after the evidence afforded by its incidents of the mythical character of the whole, is the subtle suggestion of the sense of guilt overpowering the brothers. It is supposed to be some twenty years since the disappearance of Joseph, and all the family regard him as dead. The brothers have no suspicion that the man whom they find in charge of the distribution of food in Egypt has any other relation to them than any lordly officer in that position would have. But their rough and suspicious treatment awakens memory of the wronged brother, and they at once attribute it to their guilt concerning him. So when the money is found in the sack, they are alarmed at an incident trivial in itself, as an omen of evil, — as something that God had done unto them.

There is much pathos in the old father's sense of bereavement, but the slaying of Reuben's sons, if any harm should come to Benjamin, could hardly be regarded as a comfort or a satisfactory indemnity in a tale of real life. The story, with the exception of interpolated fragments here inclosed in brackets, appears to be from the version which speaks of Jacob, and not of Israel, as the paternal patriarch, and gives Reuben instead of Judah a prominent part.

[XLII]

Now Jacob saw that there was grain in Egypt, and Jacob said unto his sons, Why do ye look one upon another? And he said, Behold, I have heard that there is grain in Egypt; get you down thither, and buy for us from thence, that we may live, and not die. And Joseph's ten brethren went down to buy grain from Egypt. But Benjamin, Joseph's brother, Jacob sent not with his brethren; for he said, Lest peradventure mischief befall him. [And the sons of Israel came to buy among those that came, for the famine was in the land of Canaan.]

And Joseph was the governor over the land; he it was that sold to all the people of the land; and Joseph's brethren came, and bowed down themselves to him with their faces to the earth. And Joseph saw his brethren, and he knew them, but made himself strange unto them, and spake roughly with them; and he said unto them, Whence come ye? And they said, From the land of Canaan to buy food. And Joseph knew his brethren, but they knew not him.

And Joseph remembered the dreams which he dreamed of them, and said unto them, Ye are spies; to see the nakedness of the land ye are come. And they said unto him, Nay, my lord, but to buy food are thy servants come. We are all one man's sons; we are true men, thy servants are no spies. And he said unto them, Nay, but to see the nakedness of the land ye are come. And they said, We thy servants are twelve brethren, the sons of one man in the land of Canaan; and, behold, the youngest is this day with our father, and one is not.

And Joseph said unto them, That is it that I spake unto you, saying, Ye are spies; hereby ye shall be proved; by the life of Pharaoh ye shall not go forth hence, except your youngest brother come hither. Send one of you, and let him fetch your brother, and ye shall be bound, that your words may be proved, whether there be truth in you; or else by the life of Pharaoh surely ye are spies. And he put them all together into ward three days. And Joseph said unto them the third day, This do, and live, for I fear God; if ye be true men, let one of your brethren be bound in your prison house; but go ye, carry grain for the famine of your houses, and bring your youngest brother unto me; so shall your words be verified, and ye shall not die. And they did so.

And they said one to another, We are verily guilty concerning our brother, in that we saw the distress of his soul, when he besought us, and we would not hear; therefore is this distress come upon us. And Reuben answered them, saying, Spake I not unto you, saying, Do not sin against the child; and ye would not hear? therefore also, behold, his blood is required. And they knew not that Joseph understood them; for there was an interpreter between them. And he turned himself about from them, and wept; and he returned to them, and spake to them, and took Simeon from among them, and bound him before their eyes.

Then Joseph commanded to fill their vessels with grain, and to restore every man's money into his sack, and to give them provision for the way; and thus was it done unto them. And they laded their asses with their grain, and departed thence.

[And as one of them opened his sack to give his ass provender in the lodging place, he espied his money; and, behold, it was in the mouth of his sack. And he said unto his brethren, My money is restored; and, lo, it is even in my sack; and their heart failed them, and they turned trembling one to another, saying, What is this that God hath done unto us?]

And they came unto Jacob their father unto the land of Canaan, and told him all that had befallen them; saying, The man, the lord of the land, spake roughly with us, and took us for spies of the country. And we said unto him, We are true men; we are no spies; we be twelve brethren, sons of our father; one is not, and the youngest is this day with our father in the land of Canaan. And the man, the lord of the land, said unto us, Hereby shall I know that ye are true men; leave one of your brethren with me, and take grain for the famine of your houses, and go your way, and bring your youngest brother unto me; then shall I know that ye are no spies, but that ye are true men; so will I deliver you your brother, and ye shall traffick in the land.

And it came to pass as they emptied their sacks, that, behold, every man's bundle of money was in his sack; and when they and their father saw their bundles of money, they were afraid. And Jacob their father said unto them, Me have ye bereaved of my children; Joseph is not, and Simeon is not, and ye will take Benjamin away; all these things are against me. And Reuben spake unto his father, saying, Slay my two sons, if I bring him not to thee; deliver him into my hand, and I will bring him to thee again. And he said, My son shall not go down with you; for his brother is dead, and he only is left; if mischief befall him by the way in which ye go, then shall ye bring down my gray hairs with sorrow to Sheol.

XXXVI

THE SECOND JOURNEY TO EGYPT

In the account of the second journey of the ten brothers — Benjamin taking the place of Simeon — into Egypt, it is Judah that appears in the character of surety for the safety of the youngest, and later offers himself as a bondman to Joseph "instead of the lad," while Reuben is not referred to by name. We notice also that the father is designated only by the personal name of Israel, and Joseph speaks of himself as "your brother whom ye sold into Egypt." This indicates the same source as the material in Chapter xxxvii. which represented Judah as saving Joseph from death by the device of selling him to a passing caravan of Ishmaelites from whom he was bought by Pharaoh's captain of the guard and keeper of the prison, and not from that which made Reuben the rescuer by the device of casting the lad into a dry "pit" from which he was "stolen away" by Midianite merchantmen, and in which Reuben also appeared as the chief spokesman of the brothers in the sequel.

We have noticed also that in the narrative of the first visit to Egypt, in which Reuben is the leading character, it is said that only one sack was opened at the "lodging place" on the return, and the money was found in the others after the brothers reached home. But here they are represented as telling Joseph's steward that when they came to the lodging place they opened their sacks, "and every man's money was in the mouth of his sack." There are, indeed, traces of blending with this story some elements from the other.

First, the brothers are described as appearing without ceremony before Joseph, who saw Benjamin and gave orders to the steward to bring them into the house and make ready for dinner, which was done, and thereupon, in their alarm, they explained about the money. But this is followed by a different description of their being brought by a "man" to Joseph's house, where they were to wait for his appearance, having "heard that they should eat bread there." When Joseph presented himself, they prostrated themselves instead of standing before him, and he graciously inquired after their father and "lifted up his eyes and saw Benjamin." The result of the banquet which followed is more strongly stated in the original than in our familiar translation.

The account of sending the brothers away after this surprising treatment, and bringing them back by the device of the apparently stolen divining cup, is of the simple fairy-tale order; but in the pathetic pleading of Judah before Joseph in behalf of Benjamin there is something strangely expressive of the relation of the tribes at the time when the story must have originated. The main ethnic purpose is kept in view, of accounting for the migration of the Israelites into Egypt, where their bondage had long been a matter of dim tradition, and of representing the ancestors of the Northern tribes as having gone down first and acquired a degree of favor and power that made them the saviours of the rest. But the story of Joseph's superior position, his graciousness to the brethren who came to him humbly for relief in time of distress, and his peculiar affection for Benjamin, tells in mythic language of a time when the Northern Kingdom was strong after Jeroboam's secession, and that of the South was humiliated; when it was a question of detaching Benjamin from Judah, and joining it to Ephraim, and possibly of subjugating Judah itself, and when the magnanimity of the Northern realm, which had the favor and support of Egypt, saved the Southern tribes from extinction.

The passage near the end of the following extract, which is put in brackets, describing Joseph's disclosure of himself to his brothers, is taken from the other version of the story than that mainly drawn upon, evidently for the sake of the statement of divine purpose which it contains.

[XLIII–XLV 16]

And the famine was sore in the land. And it came to pass, when they had eaten up the grain which they had brought out of Egypt, their father said unto them, Go again, buy us a little food. And Judah spake unto him, saying, The man did solemnly protest unto us, saying, Ye shall not see my face, except your brother be with you. If thou wilt send our brother with us, we will go down and buy thee food; but if thou wilt not send him, we will not go down, for the man said unto us, Ye shall not see my face except your brother be with you.

And Israel said, Wherefore dealt ye so ill with me, as to tell the man whether ye had yet a brother? And they said, The man asked straitly concerning ourselves, and concerning our kindred, saying, Is your father yet alive? have ye another brother? and we told him according to the tenor of these words. Could we in any wise know that he would say, Bring your brother down?

And Judah said unto Israel his father, Send the lad with me, and we will arise and go; that we may live, and not die, both we, and thou, and also our little ones. I will be surety for him; of my hand shalt thou require him; if I bring him not unto thee, and set him before thee, then let me bear the blame for ever; for except we had lingered, surely we had now returned a second time.

And their father Israel said unto them, If it be so now, do this; take of the choice fruits of the land in your vessels, and carry down the man a present, a little balm, and a little honey, spicery and myrrh, nuts, and almonds; and take double money in your hand; and the money that was returned in the mouth of your sacks carry again in your hand; peradventure it was an oversight; take also your brother, and arise, go again unto the man; and God Almighty (*El Shaddai*) give you mercy before the man, that he may release unto you your other brother and Benjamin. And if I be bereaved of my children, I am bereaved.

And the men took that present, and they took double money in their hand, and Benjamin; and rose up, and went down to Egypt, and stood before Joseph. And when Joseph saw Benjamin with them, he said to the steward of his house, Bring the men into the house, and slay, and make ready; for the men shall dine with me at noon. And the man did as Joseph bade; and the man brought the men into Joseph's house. And the men were afraid, because they were brought into Joseph's house; and they said, Because of the money that was returned in our sacks at the first time are we brought in; that he may seek occasion against us, and fall upon us, and take us for bondmen, and our asses.

And they came near to the steward of Joseph's house, and they spake unto him at the door of the house, and said, Oh my lord, we came indeed down at the first time to buy food; and it came to pass, when we came to the lodging place, that we opened our sacks, and, behold, every man's money was in the mouth of his sack, our money in full weight, and we have brought it again in our hand. And other money have we brought down in our hand to buy food; we know not who put our money in our sacks. And he said, Peace be to you, fear not; your God, and the God of your father, hath given you treasure in your sacks; I had your money. And he brought Simeon out unto them.

And the man brought the men into Joseph's house, and gave them water, and they washed their feet; and he gave their asses provender. And they made ready the present against Joseph came at noon, for they heard that they should eat bread there. And when Joseph came home, they brought him the present which was in their hand into the house, and bowed down themselves to him to the earth. And he asked them of their welfare, and said, Is your father well, the old man of whom ye spake? Is he yet alive? And they said, Thy servant our father is well, he is yet alive. And they bowed the head, and made obeisance.

And he lifted up his eyes, and saw Benjamin his brother, his mother's son, and said, Is this your youngest brother, of whom ye spake unto me? And he said, God be gracious unto thee, my son. And Joseph made haste; for his bowels did yearn upon his brother, and he sought where to weep; and he entered into his chamber, and wept there. And he washed his face, and came out; and he refrained himself, and said, Set on bread.

And they set on for him by himself, and for them by themselves, and for the Egyptians, which did eat with him, by themselves, because the Egyptians might not eat bread with the Hebrews; for that is an abomination unto the Egyptians. · And they sat before him, the firstborn according to his birthright, and the youngest according to his youth; and the men marvelled one with another. And he took and sent messes unto them from before him; but Benjamin's mess was five times so much as any of theirs. And they drank, and were drunken with him.

And he commanded the steward of his house, saying, Fill the men's sacks with food, as much as they can carry, and put every man's money in his sack's mouth. And put my cup, the silver cup, in the sack's mouth of the youngest, and his grain money. And he did according to the word that Joseph had spoken. As soon as the morning was light, the men were sent away, they and their asses.

When they were gone out of the city, and

were not yet far off, Joseph said unto his steward, Up, follow after the men; and when thou dost overtake them, say unto them, Wherefore have ye rewarded evil for good? Is not this it in which my lord drinketh, and whereby he indeed divineth? ye have done evil in so doing. And he overtook them, and he spake unto them these words. And they said unto him, Wherefore speaketh my lord such words as these? God forbid that thy servants should do such a thing. Behold, the money, which we found in our sacks' mouths, we brought again unto thee out of the land of Canaan; how then should we steal out of thy lord's house silver or gold? With whomsoever of thy servants it be found, let him die, and we also will be my lord's bondmen.

And he said, Now also let it be according unto your words; he with whom it is found shall be my bondman, and ye shall be blameless. Then they hasted, and took down every man his sack to the ground, and opened every man his sack. And he searched, and began at the eldest, and left at the youngest; and the cup was found in Benjamin's sack. Then they rent their clothes, and laded every man his ass, and returned to the city.

And Judah and his brethren came to Joseph's house, and he was yet there; and they fell before him on the ground. And Joseph said unto them, What deed is this that ye have done? know ye not that such a man as I can indeed divine? And Judah said, What shall we say unto my lord? what shall we speak? or how shall we clear ourselves? God hath found out the iniquity of thy servants. Behold, we are my lord's bondmen, both we, and he also in whose hand the cup is found. And he said, God forbid that I should do so; the man in whose hand the cup is found, he shall be my bondman; but as for you, get you up in peace unto your father.

Then Judah came near unto him, and said, Oh my lord, let thy servant, I pray thee, speak a word in my lord's ears, and let not thine anger burn against thy servant, for thou art even as Pharaoh. My lord asked his servants, saying, Have ye a father, or a brother? And we said unto my lord, We have a father, an old man, and a child of his old age, a little one; and his brother is dead, and he alone is left of his mother, and his father loveth him. And thou saidst unto thy servants, Bring him down unto me, that I may set mine eyes upon him. And we said unto my lord, The lad cannot leave his father; for if he should leave his father, his father would die. And thou saidst unto thy servants, Except your youngest brother come down with you, ye shall see my face no more. And it came to pass when we came up unto thy servant my father, we told him the words of my lord.

And our father said, Go again, buy us a little food. And we said, We cannot go down; if our youngest brother be with us, then will we go down, for we may not see the man's face, except our youngest brother be with us. And thy servant my father said unto us, Ye know that my wife bare me two sons; and the one went out from me, and I said, Surely he is torn in pieces; and I have not seen him since; and if ye take this one also from me, and mischief befall him, ye shall bring down my gray hairs with sorrow to Sheol. Now therefore when I come to thy servant my father, and the lad be not with us; seeing that his life is bound up in the lad's life, it shall come to pass, when he seeth that the lad is not with us, that he will die; and thy servants shall bring down the gray hairs of thy servant our father with sorrow to Sheol. For thy servant became surety for the lad unto my father, saying, If I bring him not unto thee, then shall I bear the blame to my father forever. Now therefore, let thy servant, I pray thee, abide instead of the lad a bondman to my lord; and let the lad go up with his brethren. For how shall I go up to my father, and the lad be not with me? lest I see the evil that shall come on my father.

Then Joseph could not refrain himself before all them that stood by him; and he cried, Cause every man to go out from me. And there stood no man with him, while Joseph made himself known unto his brethren. And he wept aloud; and the Egyptians heard, and the house of Pharaoh heard.

[And Joseph said unto his brethren, I am Joseph; doth my father yet live? And his brethren could not answer him; for they were troubled at his presence. And Joseph said unto his brethren,

Come near to me, I pray you. And they came near. And he said, I am Joseph your brother, whom ye sold into Egypt. And now be not grieved nor angry with yourselves, that ye sold me hither, for God did send me before you to preserve life. For these two years hath the famine been in the land; and there are yet five years in which there shall be neither plowing nor harvest. And God sent me before you to preserve you a remnant in the earth, and to save you alive by a great deliverance. So now it was not you that sent me hither, but God; and he hath made me a father to Pharaoh, and lord of all his house, and ruler over all the land of Egypt.

Haste ye, and go up to my father, and say unto him, Thus saith thy son Joseph, God hath made me lord of all Egypt; come down unto me, tarry not, and thou shalt dwell in the land of Goshen, and thou shalt be near unto me, thou, and thy children, and thy children's children, and thy flocks, and thy herds, and all that thou hast; and there will I nourish thee, for there are yet five years of famine, lest thou come to poverty, thou, and thy household, and all that thou hast. And, behold, your eyes see, and the eyes of my brother Benjamin, that it is my mouth that speaketh unto you. And ye shall tell my father of all my glory in Egypt, and of all that ye have seen; and ye shall haste and bring down my father hither.]

And he fell upon his brother Benjamin's neck, and wept; and Benjamin wept upon his neck.

And he kissed all his brethren, and wept upon them; and after that his brethren talked with him. And the fame thereof was heard in Pharaoh's house, saying, Joseph's brethren are come; and it pleased Pharaoh well, and his servants.

XXXVII

JACOB'S MIGRATION

AGAIN the charming simplicity of the fairy tale, with Joseph in the character of the kindly godmother and Pharaoh as the benignant dispenser of endless favors! The mighty potentate of Egypt, who has raised a Hebrew slave to the highest place of power and confidence in his realm, personally sends for the aged patriarch in that indefinite home, "the land of Canaan," to come down with all his family and share the good things of Egypt, leaving all possessions behind as of no account. Wagons are sent and gifts are bestowed by the lordly brother, special favors being lavished upon little Benjamin.

We lose sight of the awful famine with five years still to run, in visions of "the fat of the land," and we do not mind that twenty asses, however richly laden, were an inadequate cavalcade for the supplies on so long a journey and return, through a country which the later Israelites found it so hard to traverse. We do not think how the wagons are to get through that perilous wilderness, parched and burnt with two years of drought already.

It is all as easy as an Arabian tale, and only a question of breaking the joyful news to the incredulous old father and bringing him in all haste to the land of plenty and of Joseph's glory. He bethinks him on his departure of Isaac's God, whose altar is at Beersheba, and there he gets a promise in the visions of the night that the divinity of his father will accompany him to the strange land and bring up his offspring again in the time to come to be a great nation. It is evidently the God of Isaac only, and in the long interval Canaan will be left in sole possession of its own deities, and not till Moses appears as a deliverer will he concern himself even with the fate of Israel in Egypt. Is it in the wilderness about Mount Sinai that he is to lurk in the mean time, waiting the growth of the promised nation? However it may be, Jacob is got into Egypt and "all his family with him." The account of the migration is of mixed material, that from the secondary source being put in brackets in the text below.

It is almost with a shock that we pass from this exquisite picture to the prosaic genealogy of the children of Israel which the compiler saw fit to introduce here, doubtless from the Elohist document of which we have seemed to lose sight for some time. The shock does not come alone from the abrupt transition. We have seen Reuben offering the sacrifice of his "two sons," if Benjamin should not be brought back in safety; but now we find him with four sons, whose names have a strange suggestion of antique geography. Simeon and Levi have appeared once before as mature men in the bloody episode of Shechem, and now they have their sons who seem also to be geographical expressions. We are reminded again of Judah's family history by the names of his offspring, while the mention of Leah's other sons and those of the handmaids carries us back to the Jacob legend, so different from that which has lately charmed us.

But here is Benjamin, the tender lad, the "child of his old age, a little one," appearing as the father of ten children. Perhaps we need not be surprised, for was he not born on the journey from Paddanaram, when Rachel died, and when his father was some sixty years old, now according to his own statement to Pharaoh about seventy years ago? The defective arithmetic, which appears also in the enumeration of the family, does not matter. What has arithmetic or other hard fact to do with the story of Joseph and his little brother, which has delighted the world for centuries? No more than with the nightly adventures of Haroun al Raschid in the "golden prime."

[XLV 17–XLVI 27]

And Pharaoh said unto Joseph, Say unto thy brethren, This do ye: lade your beasts, and go, get you unto the land of Canaan; and take your father and your households, and come unto me; and I will give you the good of the land of Egypt, and ye shall eat the fat of the land. Now thou art commanded, this do ye; take you wagons out of the land of Egypt for your little ones, and for your wives, and bring your father, and come. Also regard not your stuff; for the good of all the land of Egypt is yours. And the sons of Israel did so; and Joseph gave them wagons, according to the commandment of Pharaoh, and gave them provision for the way.

[To all of them he gave each man changes of raiment; but to Benjamin he gave three hundred pieces of silver, and five changes of raiment. And to his father he sent after this manner; ten asses laden with the good things of Egypt, and ten she-asses laden with grain and bread and victual for his father by the way. So he sent his brethren away, and they departed; and he said unto them, See that ye fall not out by the way. And they went up out of Egypt, and came into the land of Canaan unto Jacob their father.]

And they told him, saying, Joseph is yet alive, and he is ruler over all the land of Egypt. And his heart fainted, for he believed them not. And they told him all the words of Joseph, which he had said unto them; and when he saw the wagons which Joseph had sent to carry him, the spirit of Jacob their father revived; and Israel said, It is enough, Joseph my son is yet alive; I will go and see him before I die.

And Israel took his journey with all that he had, and came to Beersheba, and offered sacrifices unto the God of his father Isaac. And God spake unto Israel in the visions of the night, and said, Jacob, Jacob. And he said, Here am I. And he said, I am God, the God of thy father; fear not to go down into Egypt, for I will there make of thee a great nation; I will go down with thee into Egypt, and I will also surely bring thee up again; and Joseph shall put his hand upon thine eyes. And Jacob rose up from Beersheba; and the sons of Israel carried Jacob their father, and their little ones, and their wives, in the wagons which Pharaoh had sent to carry him.

[And they took their cattle, and their goods, which they had gotten in the land of Canaan, and came into Egypt, Jacob, and all his family with him; his sons, and his sons' sons with him, his daughters, and his sons' daughters, and all his family brought he with him into Egypt.]

And these are the names of the children of Israel, which came into Egypt, Jacob and his sons: Reuben, Jacob's firstborn. And the sons of Reuben; Hanoch, and Pallu, and Hezron, and Carmi. And the sons of Simeon; Jemuel, and Jamin, and Ohad, and Jachin, and Zohar, and Shaul the son of a Canaanitish woman. And the sons of Levi; Gershon, Kohath, and Merari. And the sons of Judah; Er, and Onan, and Shelah, and Perez, and Zerah; [but Er and Onan died in the land of Canaan.] And the sons of Perez were Hezron and Hamul. And the sons of Issachar; Tola, and Puvah, and Iob, and Shimron. And the sons of Zebulun; Sered, and Elon, and Jahleel. These are the sons of Leah, which she bare unto Jacob in Paddan-aram, with his daughter Dinah; all the souls of his sons and his daughters were thirty and three.

And the sons of Gad; Ziphion, and Haggi, Shuni, and Ezbon, Eri, and Arodi, and Areli. And the sons of Asher; Imnah, and Ishvah, and Ishvi, and Beriah, and Serah their sister: and the sons of Beriah; Heber, and Malchiel. These are the sons of Zilpah, which Laban gave to Leah his daughter, and these she bare unto Jacob, even sixteen souls.

The sons of Rachel Jacob's wife; Joseph and Benjamin. And unto Joseph in the land of Egypt were born Manasseh and Ephraim, which Asenath the daughter of Poti-phera priest of On bare unto him. And the sons of Benjamin; Bela, and

Becher, and Ashbel, Gera, and Naaman, Ehi, and Rosh, Muppim, and Huppim, and Ard. These are the sons of Rachel, which were born to Jacob; all the souls were fourteen.

And the sons of Dan; Hushim. And the sons of Naphtali; Jahzeel, and Guni, and Jezer, and Shillem. These are the sons of Bilhah, which Laban gave unto Rachel his daughter, and these she bare unto Jacob; all the souls were seven.

All the souls that came with Jacob into Egypt, which came out of his loins, besides Jacob's sons' wives, all the souls were threescore and six; and the sons of Joseph, which were born to him in Egypt, were two souls: all the souls of the house of Jacob, which came into Egypt, were threescore and ten.

x

XXXVIII

SETTLED IN EGYPT

Nothing but the fixed impressions which have been produced by traditional views of this composition, would excuse a constant reference to the evidence which it contains within itself of its utterly unhistorical character and purpose. But for those impressions the evidence would be obvious and readily accepted. Now it seems to be necessary to direct close attention to it.

The subjoined passage contains that evidence not only in the innate improbability of its incidents, and their inconsistency with other parts of the general narrative, but in the process which we have tried to make familiar to the reader's mind of a blending of diverse elements in the story. When Joseph disclosed his identity to his brothers, we are told that he bade them make haste and bring their father down to the land of Goshen, with their families and their flocks and herds, that they might be nourished through the remaining five years of famine, for he was "lord of all Egypt."

In what immediately followed Pharaoh appeared

as telling Joseph what to say to his brethren and as offering to their father and their households "the good of the land of Egypt." They were to leave all behind and come to Pharaoh to "eat the fat of the land." There is no suggestion of the famine or of dwelling apart in Goshen, but at the close of the story of the migration we are told that they "took their cattle and their goods." The possession of these during the period of dire stress, and taking them through that desolate wilderness scorched for two years by drought, would seem strange in any relation of presumed facts.

We have had a complete account of this migration, including a visit to the altar at Beersheba, the arrival in Egypt, and an enumeration of the "souls of the house of Jacob" that settled there. But here we are suddenly set back upon an account which represents Jacob as sending Judah on ahead to show the way to Goshen, and Joseph as coming up to meet him in his chariot. The latter is then to tell Pharaoh of their coming with their flocks and herds, and they are to ask the privilege of dwelling in Goshen, because they were shepherds, and every shepherd was an "abomination unto the Egyptians." Of this state of feeling in Egypt in ancient times there really seems to be no proof, and its own people were largely agricultural, if not pastoral.

With the usual magic of such tales, Joseph has then only to "go in" and tell Pharaoh about it, taking five of his brothers with him, and we hardly stop to wonder at the plea that they had come down for pasture for their flocks, because the famine was "sore in the land of Canaan." We had supposed it to be equally sore in all the land of Egypt, and that there were to be five years more during which flocks and herds would be a burden and the people must be fed from government supplies. It seems strange, too, if Goshen was "the best of the land of Egypt" and capable of sustaining flocks and herds, that it was not occupied by the Egyptians who had been suffering from famine for two years.

The paragraph which represents Joseph as bringing his father before Pharaoh is evidently from another source. It is in a different tone and manner, and apparently belongs to the narrative which brought Jacob so promptly into Egypt, and not merely to a meeting place on the border in the land of Goshen. It is Joseph again who has the disposal of affairs, and the name given to the land placed in possession of his family is Rameses, and not Goshen. It doubtless designated the same region, which lay between the Nile Valley and Arabia Petræa, and was the actual place of sojourn of the Semitic Nomads who were driven over the border by dearth of pasturage in a time of prolonged drought.

[XLVI 28-XLVII 12]

And he sent Judah before him unto Joseph, to shew the way before him into Goshen; and they came into the land of Goshen. And Joseph made ready his chariot, and went up to meet Israel his father, to Goshen; and he presented himself unto him, and fell on his neck, and wept on his neck a good while. And Israel said unto Joseph, Now let me die, since I have seen thy face, that thou art yet alive.

And Joseph said unto his brethren, and unto his father's house, I will go up, and tell Pharaoh, and will say unto him, My brethren, and my father's house, which were in the land of Canaan, are come unto me; and the men are shepherds, for they have been keepers of cattle; and they have brought their flocks, and their herds, and all that they have. And it shall come to pass, when Pharaoh shall call you, and shall say, What is your occupation? that ye shall say, Thy servants have been keepers of cattle from our youth even until now, both we, and our fathers, that ye may dwell in the land of Goshen; for every shepherd is an abomination unto the Egyptians.

Then Joseph went in and told Pharaoh, and said, My father and my brethren, and their flocks, and their herds, and all that they have, are come out of the land of Canaan; and, behold, they are in the land of Goshen. And from among his brethren he took five men, and presented them unto Pharaoh. And Pharaoh said unto his brethren, What is your occupation? And they said unto Pharaoh, Thy servants are shepherds, both we, and our fathers. And they said unto Pharaoh, To sojourn in the land are we come; for there is no pasture for thy servants' flocks; for the famine is sore in the land of Canaan; now therefore, we pray thee, let thy servants dwell in the land of Goshen. And Pharaoh spake unto Joseph, saying, Thy father and thy brethren are come unto thee; the land of Egypt is before thee; in the best of the land make thy father and thy brethren to dwell; in the land of Goshen let them dwell; and if thou knowest any able men among them, then make them rulers over my cattle.

[And Joseph brought in Jacob his father, and set him before Pharaoh, and Jacob blessed Pharaoh. And Pharaoh said unto Jacob, How many are the days of the years of thy life? And Jacob said unto Pharaoh, The days of the years of my pilgrimage are an hundred and thirty years: few and evil have been the days of the years of my life, and they have not attained unto the days of the years of the life of my fathers in the days of their pilgrimage. And Jacob blessed Pharaoh, and went out from the presence of Pharaoh. And Joseph placed his father and his brethren, and gave them a possession in the land of Egypt, (*in the best of the land, in the land of Rameses, as Pharaoh had commanded.*) And Joseph nourished his father, and his brethren, and all his father's household, with bread, according to their families.]

XXXIX

STRANGE RESULTS OF FAMINE

It is believed to be a historical fact that in the days of the great Rameses the ownership of land in Egypt was chiefly, if not solely, in the hands of the king and his officers and soldiers, and of the priests, and that the mass of the people were reduced to a state of virtual serfdom and dependence on the government. The payment of a "fifth" for the use of the land may have been a "statute."

We have here an account of something like this state of things being brought about as the result of the great famine under the administration of Joseph. It seems to be part of the scheme for magnifying the greatness of Joseph, and is characteristic of the Hebrew manner of accounting for conditions known or believed to exist in past times or distant lands. It is needless to point out that such a gathering up of everything by one man, as a matter of policy and of economic management during a seven years' period of absolute dearth, does not come within the range of credibility; but the account is not of a kind which would elsewhere lay any claim to credibility. It seems to be mainly the work of the compiler, and not an integral part of his material.

[XLVII 13-26]

And there was no bread in all the land; for the famine was very sore, so that the land of Egypt and the land of Canaan fainted by reason of the famine. And Joseph gathered up all the money that was found in the land of Egypt, and in the land of Canaan, for the grain which they bought; and Joseph brought the money into Pharaoh's house. And when the money was all spent in the land of Egypt, and in the land of Canaan, all the Egyptians came unto Joseph, and said, Give us bread: for why should we die in thy presence? for our money faileth. And Joseph said, Give your cattle; and I will give you for your cattle, if money fail. And they brought their cattle unto Joseph; and Joseph gave them bread in exchange for the horses, and for the flocks, and for the herds, and for the asses; and he fed them with bread in exchange for all their cattle for that year.

And when that year was ended, they came unto him the second year, and said unto him, We will not hide from my lord, how that our money is all spent, and the herds of cattle are my lord's; there is nought left in the sight of my lord, but our bodies, and our hands; wherefore should we die before thine eyes, both we and our land? buy us and our land for bread, and we and our land will be servants unto Pharaoh; and give us seed, that we may live, and not die, and that the land be not desolate. So Joseph bought all the land of Egypt for Pharaoh; for the Egyptians sold every man his field, because the famine was sore upon them; and the land became Pharaoh's.

And as for the people, he reduced them to serfdom from one end of the border of Egypt even to the other end thereof. Only the land of the priests bought he not, for the priests had a portion from Pharaoh, and did eat their portion which Pharaoh gave them; wherefore they sold not their land. Then Joseph said unto the people, Behold, I have bought you this day and your land for Pharaoh; lo, here is seed for you, and ye shall sow the land. And it shall come to pass at the ingatherings, that ye shall give a fifth unto Pharaoh, and four parts shall be your own, for seed of the field, and for your food, and for them of your households, and for food for your little ones. And they said, Thou hast saved our lives; let us find grace in the sight of my lord, and we will be Pharaoh's servants. And Joseph made it a statute concerning the land of Egypt unto this day, that Pharaoh should have the fifth; only the land of the priests alone became not Pharaoh's.

XL

ADOPTION OF THE TRIBES OF JOSEPH

AFTER the foregoing passage the compiler introduced a concise statement of the settlement of "Israel" in the land of Egypt where they "multiplied exceedingly," and followed it with a fragment from the Elohist document giving the age of "Jacob" at the time of his death. Reverting to the material which used the name Israel, he gave an account of the last days of the patriarch, when he summoned Joseph and made him swear that he would bury him in the burial place of his fathers in the land of Canaan. This was the last act of consecration of the possession of that land by his posterity, whose writers were careful to represent that the bones of their ancestors rested in its soil, in ground solemnly acquired and devoted to that purpose. The form of oath euphemistically expressed in the text, like that exacted of his servant by Abraham with reference to the marriage of Isaac, appears to have been a relic of the time when a peculiar sacredness was attached to the natural power and agencies of reproduction.

Apparently this account of the oath of Joseph originally ended with the death of "Israel," but the compiler had another episode of his last days to introduce, — that of adopting Ephraim and Manasseh into the family of tribes, by the process of blessing the sons of Joseph. He began this with an extract from the Elohist (in brackets below), which represents Joseph as being informed of the sickness of his father and as taking his two sons to the bedside. Only these, born before Jacob went into Egypt, are adopted, and it is implied that Joseph had other offspring which was not of Israel. The account is a recognition of supposed facts as to the relation of the tribes. From the Judean point of view, Ephraim and Manasseh, powerful as they had become, were regarded as comparatively alien in origin and as "added" or adopted by Israel. The abrupt reminder of the premature death of Rachel seems to be intended as an explanation of the adoption of the sons of Joseph on the same footing with the oldest of his brothers, on the ground that the chance of other direct progeny in that line had been cut off, and Joseph himself had passed out of the family.

The actual account of the blessing after this

preliminary statement is from the other, or Jehovist, source. There is in it a certain analogy with Isaac's blessing of his two sons, in the old man's blindness, and in the preference given to the younger over the older. It lacks the element of deception and the actual exclusion of the older branch from the heritage, but it embodies the ethnic facts as to the relation of Ephraim and Manasseh to each other and to the other tribes, as the story of Isaac's blessing embodied those of the relations of Israel and Edom. The elements of the myth are of a more kindly sort as belonging to the internal affairs of Israel. The description gives the impression that "the lads," Joseph's sons, are young children, but they have both been represented as born sometime before the famine, which had lasted two years when Jacob came into Egypt, now seventeen years ago. This is much less incongruous than the sudden appearance of the "lad" Benjamin as the father of ten sons.

But, as we have said, this is a representation of ethnic facts and relations as they were understood in the writer's time, and not a family history. The Ephraimites already possessed that "portion," or mountain slope (Shechem), given to Joseph above his brethren; but that Jacob had taken it from the Amorite with his sword and his bow was merely a symbolical statement of its conquest by the Israelites. We have had no account of warlike acquisitions by Jacob, and in the legend he has displayed none of the qualities of a conqueror. It was Israel as a people that had made the conquest and allotted the portion to the Josephite tribes, and Joseph was never brought again to the land of his fathers except in the same ethnic sense. We are to look at these statements, as their writer did, from the point of view of accomplished events.

[XLVII 27–XLVIII]

And Israel dwelt in the land of Egypt, in the land of Goshen; and they gat them possessions therein, and were fruitful, and multiplied exceedingly. [And Jacob lived in the land of Egypt seventeen years; so the days of Jacob, the years of his life, were an hundred forty and seven years.] And the time drew near that Israel must die; and he called his son Joseph, and said unto him, If now I have found grace in thy sight, put, I pray thee, thy hand under my thigh, and deal kindly and truly with me. Bury me not, I pray thee, in Egypt; but when I sleep with my fathers, thou shalt carry me out of Egypt, and bury me in their buryingplace. And he said, I will do as thou hast said. And he said, Swear unto me: and he sware unto him. And Israel bowed himself upon the bed's head.

[And it came to pass after these things, that one said to Joseph, Behold, thy father is sick; and he took with him his two sons, Manasseh and Ephraim. And one told Jacob, and said, Behold, thy son Joseph cometh unto thee: *and Israel strengthened himself, and sat upon the bed.* And Jacob said unto Joseph, God Almighty (*El Shaddai*) appeared unto me at Luz in the land of Canaan, and blessed me, and said unto me, Behold, I will make thee fruitful, and multiply thee, and I will make of thee a union of peoples; and will give this land to thy posterity after thee for an everlasting possession. And now thy two sons, which were born unto thee in the land of Egypt before I came unto thee into Egypt, are mine; Ephraim and Manasseh, even as Reuben and Simeon, shall be mine. And thy issue, which thou begettest after them, shall be thine; they shall be called after the name of their brethren in their inheritance. And as for me, when I came from Paddan, Rachel died by me in the land of Canaan in the way, when there was still some way to come unto Ephrath; and I buried her there in the way to Ephrath (the same is Beth-lehem).]

And Israel beheld Joseph's sons, and said, Who are these? And Joseph said unto his father, They are my sons, whom God hath given me here. And he said, Bring them, I pray thee, unto me, and I will bless them. Now the eyes of Israel were dim for age, so that he could not see. And he brought them near unto him; and he kissed them, and embraced them. And Israel said unto Joseph, I had not thought to see thy face; and, lo, God hath let me see thy children also. And Joseph brought them out from between his knees; and he bowed himself with his face to the earth.

And Joseph took them both, Ephraim in his right hand toward Israel's left hand, and Manasseh in his left hand toward Israel's right hand, and brought them near unto him. And Israel stretched out his right hand, and laid it upon Ephraim's head, who was the younger, and his left hand upon Manasseh's head, guiding his hands wittingly; for Manasseh was the firstborn. And he blessed Joseph, and said, The God before whom my fathers Abraham and Isaac did walk, the God which hath fed me all my life long unto this day, the angel which hath redeemed me from all evil, bless the lads; and let my name be named on them, and the name of my fathers Abraham and Isaac; and let them grow into a multitude in the midst of the earth.

And when Joseph saw that his father laid his right hand upon the head of Ephraim, it displeased him; and he held up his father's hand, to remove it from Ephraim's head unto Manasseh's head. And Joseph said unto his father, Not so, my father, for this is the firstborn; put thy right hand upon his head. And his father refused, and said, I know it, my son, I know it; he also shall become a people, and he also shall be great; howbeit his younger brother shall be greater than he, and his progeny shall become a multitude of nations. And he blessed them that day, saying, In thee shall Israel bless, saying, God make thee as Ephraim and as Manasseh; and he set Ephraim before Manasseh.

And Israel said unto Joseph, Behold, I die, but God shall be with you, and bring you again unto the land of your fathers. Moreover I have given to thee one mountain slope (*shechem*) above thy brethren, which I took out of the hand of the Amorite with my sword and with my bow.

XLI

POETICAL DESCRIPTION OF THE TRIBES

Nearly the whole of the forty-ninth chapter of Genesis is taken up with a poetical *résumé* of the characteristics of the tribes of Israel at a certain period of their history. It is of extreme interest as betraying even more clearly than the preceding narratives the fact that the names with which we have been dealing represent in their origin symbolical personifications of the tribes. It is introduced with the statement, that it is what Jacob told his sons would befall them "in the latter days," and the compiler followed it with the declaration that it related to the tribes of Israel, and was what their father "spake unto them and blessed them." It is generally spoken of as a "blessing" or benediction, but it has little of that quality except for Joseph. It is partly in the form of prediction, but more of description or characterization.

The origin of this poetical production is a matter of conjecture, or of inference. The compiler found it among his varied material, with or without the introductory statement, and likelihood favors the supposition that it was one of many ancient chants, in which tales, traditions, and descriptions were embodied at a time when they were transmitted orally, and constant repetition in rhythmical forms served to keep them in memory until they finally came to be written down. When its substance had been drawn into prose narratives, after writing came into use, most of the primitive ballad literature was lost.

The time reflected in this poem appears to be after the complete establishment of the kingdom, which included all the tribes, and before its division into two rival and often hostile powers, but its general tone is strongly Ephraimite, while recognizing the predominance at the time of Judah.

Reuben was regarded as the oldest of the tribes, which had lost the pre-eminence it once held. The symbolism seems to imply that this was due to presumption in usurping undue authority over the rest, for we know from the story of David and Absalom, and from other authority, that taking possession of the father's harem (or defiling his bed) was the supreme evidence of seizing his prerogatives. An attempt of the Reubenites to establish themselves as the ruling power may explain the enigmatical reference here to the "father's bed," and in the previous story, to one of his "concubines." At all events, Reuben lost its primacy after the conquest and practically disappeared as one of the tribes to the east of the Jordan.

The allusion to the violence of Simeon and Levi, which we have also had before in the story of Shechem, is still more enigmatical, for we are told of no event of history which explains it, but we do know that they were "scattered" in Israel. The tribe of Simeon had utterly faded out on the southern border since the conquest, and the Levites were a wandering class without territorial possessions of their own. There is no trace of recognition here of the character which they finally assumed as ministers of the national worship.

The powerful and flourishing state of Judah is recognized, and it evidently held the sceptre of power over Israel at the time pictured in the poem, which could only have been after the beginning of the Davidic dynasty. The figure of the lion's whelp may refer to the conquests over the Philistines and other enemies in the days of David, and the references to wine and milk evidently symbolize material prosperity. What means the retention of the ruler's staff until

Shiloh come? Is it an ominous intimation that Ephraim, whose most ancient fane was at or near Shiloh, harbored the expectation of obtaining the supreme sway? Though Shiloh is found only as a proper name elsewhere, some critics have been disposed to regard it as a common noun here, meaning peace, and implying that Judah was to exercise kingly power only until the country was reduced to tranquillity, when the people were to revert to the primitive freedom for which they always yearned.

Zebulun is characterized only by reference to its situation on the seaboard. Issachar was an agricultural and pastoral land of considerable richness, and is spoken of in the guise of a laborer and bearer of burdens. The name "Dan" means a judge, and there is an apparent allusion to the time when a small settlement on the Philistine border got the better of a powerful enemy for a while, and furnished one of the most famous "judges of Israel." That exploit may have raised it to the dignity of the "tribe" which afterwards settled in the North. Gad on the eastern frontier was exposed to marauding attacks, which it constantly repelled, and Asher on the rich western slope furnished dainties to the markets of Phœnicia. The nimble warriors of the heights, whence

Deborah summoned Barak, were a "hind let loose," who gave "good words," whether literally in battle songs or figuratively in giving good account of themselves, who can say? But it is to be observed of these six names of tribes, that nowhere in the patriarchal stories do the two youngest sons of Leah, or the four offspring of handmaidens, assume any personal individuality. They are mere names, or are included in the general designation of "sons of Jacob" or "brethren of Joseph," without separate identity. As tribes, they were scarcely more than "geographical expressions." They had no autonomy.

Joseph is the one upon whom the blessings of a dying father are lavished, with promise of expansion and triumph. This stamps the poem as an Ephraimite production beyond question, and suggests a time of ambitious hopes in the Northern land. But poor little Benjamin does not appear as the favorite brother of Joseph and the beloved child of his father. He personifies rather the characteristics of that violent band of warriors that made a new Sodom of Gibeah in the time of the Judges, and brought upon them the wrath of the other tribes by the outrage upon the poor Levite who tarried there with his concubine from Bethlehem-Judah.

A later and less poetical picture of the tribes is found in the so-called blessing of Moses, delivered when he was about to die in sight of the promised land, which is contained in the thirty-third chapter of Deuteronomy. It is traced in part upon the lines of the earlier composition, but breathes a kindlier spirit. Simeon has disappeared, but there is an appeal that Reuben may live, and the priestly character of Levi is recognized while the violence formerly attributed to him is forgotten. The power of Judah is much abated, while the blessing of Joseph continues, and Benjamin is referred to with kindness. It is interesting to compare the two poems, as presenting a view of the tribes at different periods after their union, and as throwing light upon the use of their names in the ethnic myths.

[XLIX 1-28]

And Jacob called unto his sons, and said: Gather yourselves together, that I may tell you that which shall befall you in the latter days.
Assemble yourselves, and hear, ye sons of Jacob;
And hearken unto Israel your father.

Reuben, thou art my firstborn, my might, and the beginning of my strength;

The pre-eminence of dignity, and the pre-eminence of power.
Boiling over as water, thou shalt not have the pre-eminence,
Because thou wentest up to thy father's bed;
Then defiledst thou it: he went up to my couch.

Simeon and Levi are brethren;
Weapons of violence are their compacts.
My soul will not come into their council;
Unto their assembly my glory shall not be united;
For in their anger they slew a man,
And in their selfwill they houghed an ox.
Cursed be their anger, for it was fierce;
And their wrath, for it was cruel:
I will divide them in Jacob,
And scatter them in Israel.

[Judah, thee shall thy brethren praise;
Thy hand shall be on the neck of thine enemies;
Thy father's sons shall bow down before thee.[1]]
Judah is a lion's whelp;
From the prey, my son, thou art returned.
He stooped down, he couched as a lion,
And as a lioness; who shall rouse him up?
The sceptre shall not depart from Judah,
Nor the ruler's staff from between his feet,
Until Shiloh come;
And unto him shall the obedience of the peoples be.

---

[1] There is a question whether these three lines have not been displaced from the reference to Joseph with a substitution of names.

Binding his foal unto the vine,
And his ass's colt unto the choice vine,
He hath washed his garments in wine,
And his vesture in the blood of grapes;
His eyes shall be red with wine,
And his teeth white with milk.

Zebulun shall dwell at the haven of the sea,
And he shall be for an haven of ships;
And his border shall be upon Zidon.

Issachar is a strong ass,
Couching down between the sheepfolds;
And he saw a resting place that it was good,
And the land that it was pleasant;
And he bowed his shoulder to bear,
And became a servant under taskwork.

[Dan shall judge his people,
As one of the tribes of Israel.]
Dan shall be a serpent in the way,
An adder in the path,
That biteth the horse's heels,
So that his rider falleth backward.
[I have waited for thy salvation, O LORD.]

Gad, a troop shall press upon him;
But he shall press upon their heel.

Out of Asher his bread shall be fat,
And he shall yield royal dainties.

Naphtali is a hind let loose;
He giveth goodly words.

Joseph is a fruitful bough,
A fruitful bough by a fountain;
His branches run over the wall.
The archers have sorely grieved him,
And shot at him, and persecuted him;
But his bow abode in strength,
And the arms of his hands were made strong,
By the hands of the Mighty One of Jacob,
(From thence is the shepherd, the rock of Israel,)
Even by the God of thy father, who shall help thee,
And by the Almighty, who shall bless thee,
With blessings of heaven above,
Blessings of the deep that coucheth beneath,
Blessings of the breasts, and of the womb.
The blessings of thy father
Have prevailed above the blessings of my progenitors
Unto the utmost bound of the everlasting hills.
They shall be on the head of Joseph,
And on the crown of the head of him that was separate from his brethren.

Benjamin is a wolf that ravineth;
In the morning he shall devour the prey,
And at even he shall divide the spoil.

All these are the twelve tribes of Israel; and this is it that their father spake unto them and blessed them; every one according to his blessing he blessed them.

XLII

THE BURIAL OF JACOB

THE beginning and end of the following passage relating to the burial of Jacob, which are put in brackets, are from the Elohist document and connect with each other. The accounts of the purchase of the cave of Machpelah and the burial there of Sarah, Abraham, and Isaac in previous chapters, are from the same source, as we have seen. The Jehovist associated Jacob mostly with Bethel and Shechem, as he associated Isaac only with Beersheba. In the account of Jacob's first going to Shechem after his return from Paddan-aram, it is said that he bought a parcel of ground there of the children of Hamor, and in the Book of Joshua it is stated that the bones of Joseph, "which the children of Israel brought up out of Egypt," they buried in that parcel of ground. In the account of Jacob's burial which follows the Elohist fragment below, the reference in the original material is probably to this place. This account is complete in itself and seems to have connected originally with what is now the end of chapter xlvii., where Jacob is said to have summoned Joseph to his death bed and made him swear to carry him out of Egypt and bury him in the "burying-place" of his fathers.

Joseph is now represented as saying that his father had made him swear to bury him in a grave which he had himself bought in the land of Canaan. It seems a little strange to find Joseph making his application to Pharaoh through intermediaries of the king's household. The embalming and the mourning appear to be according to known Egyptian custom, but the funeral cortege, with "horses and chariots," and the dignitaries of Egypt, passing through all that wilderness of Pharan, is a sharp reminder of the unreality of the whole description regarded as a matter of personal history. There is also a reminder of the fallibility of the process of deriving events from names, which was so common with the myth-makers of Israel. There was a plain, not far from Jericho east of the Jordan, which was called Abel-Mizraim, for some unknown reason, but that meant "field of the Egyptians" and not "mourning of the Egyptians." The mistaken derivation which formed the suggestion of the whole incident came from confounding Ebel, "mourning," with Abel, "field." In the old Hebrew writing no vowels were used, and it is likely that the distinction of vowel sounds was not always kept clear in oral speech. Of the perversion of the names of places on account of similarity of sound with something else there are many modern instances.

[XLIX 29-L 13]

[And he charged them, and said unto them, I am to be gathered unto my people; bury me with my fathers in the cave that is in the field of Ephron the Hittite, in the cave that is in the field of Machpelah, which is before Mamre, in the land of Canaan, which Abraham bought with the field from Ephron the Hittite for a possession of a buryingplace. There they buried Abraham and Sarah his wife; there they buried Isaac and Rebekah his wife; and there I buried Leah: the field and the cave that is therein, which was purchased from the children of Heth. And when Jacob made an end of charging his sons, he gathered up his feet into the bed, and yielded up the ghost, and was gathered unto his people.]

And Joseph fell upon his father's face, and wept upon him, and kissed him. And Joseph commanded his servants the physicians to embalm his father; and the physicians embalmed Israel. And forty days were fulfilled for him; for so are fulfilled the days of embalming; and the Egyptians wept for him threescore and ten days.

And when the days of weeping for him were past, Joseph spake unto the house of Pharaoh, saying, If now I have found grace in your eyes, speak, I pray you, in the ears of Pharaoh, saying, My father made me swear, saying, Lo, I die: in my grave which I bought for me in the land of Canaan, there shalt thou bury me. Now therefore let me go up, I pray thee, and bury my father, and I will come again.

And Pharaoh said, Go up, and bury thy father, according as he made thee swear. And Joseph went up to bury his father; and with him went up all the servants of Pharaoh, the elders of his house, and all the elders of the land of Egypt, and all the house of Joseph, and his brethren, and his father's house; only their little ones, and their flocks, and their herds, they left in the land of Goshen.

And there went up with him both chariots and horsemen, and it was a very great company. And they came to the threshing-floor of Atad, which is beyond Jordan, and there they lamented with a very great and sore lamentation; and he made a mourning for his father seven days. And when the inhabitants of the land, the Canaanites, saw the mourning in the floor of Atad, they said, This is a grievous mourning to the Egyptians: wherefore the name of it was called Abel-mizraim, which is beyond Jordan.

[And his sons did unto him according as he commanded them; for his sons carried him unto the land of Canaan, and buried him in the cave of the field of Machpelah, which Abraham bought with the field, for a possession of a buryingplace, of Ephron the Hittite, before Mamre.]

XLIII

THE END OF JOSEPH

With the completion of the story of Joseph the purpose of the patriarchal myths is fulfilled. The origin of the tribes, their characteristics and their relation to each other, have been accounted for; the sacred places of the nation have been hallowed with memories of the people's earliest ancestors; the possession of the land has been attributed to divine promise many times repeated, to early occupation, and the consecration of ancestral graves; obedience to Jehovah's commands and devotion to his worship have been made a solemn obligation through the compacts of the venerable forefathers of the Hebrew race; and finally the sojourn in Egypt, leading to the bondage and deliverance of which there had been traditions for centuries, has been explained as the result of divine care in preserving the people in a time of terrible and protracted famine.

Through the series of stories runs the exaltation of the offspring of Abraham over all other peoples, the elevation of the Israelite branch over the Ishmaelite and Edomite, and finally the glorification of the family of Joseph, constituting the kingdom of the North, in which the main substance of the myths in their original form was produced.

Joseph's mission in Egypt being fulfilled, he is represented as dying, while his brothers live on, and as making them swear to carry his bones up out of Egypt when the time of their deliverance should come. The naïve passing from the phrase "his brethren" to the "children of Israel," leads one to think that the writer was wholly conscious of the mythical quality of his narrative, and had no notion of its being received as ordinary matter of fact. Indeed, historical fact was something beyond the recognition or the conception of those ancient scribes. We notice one of the constant characteristics of their method in the general mention of Ephraim's "children" and of Manasseh's son by name, the fact being that the powerful tribe of Ephraim was never divided, whereas there was a branch of that of Manasseh known as Machirites, on the east side of the Jordan.

Another characteristic touch, indicative of a primitive moral standard in matters of truth, appears in the little episode of the reconciliation after the father's death, in which the brothers pretend that he left a dying injunction to Joseph to forgive their transgression. It would have been easy to represent the patriarch as delivering this injunction for himself, but the primitive writer and the compiler of the material alike had as little conception of literary art as of any necessity of giving a semblance of candor to their characters. The quality was not valued by their race and time.

[L 14-26]

And Joseph returned into Egypt, he, and his brethren, and all that went up with him to bury his father, after he had buried his father. And when Joseph's brethren saw that their father was dead, they said, It may be that Joseph will hate us, and will fully requite us all the evil which we did unto him.

And they sent a message unto Joseph, saying, Thy father did command before he died, saying, So shall ye say unto Joseph, Forgive, I pray thee now, the transgression of thy brethren, and their sin, for that they did unto thee evil; and now, we pray thee, forgive the transgression of the servants of the God of thy father.

And Joseph wept when they spake unto him. And his brethren also went and fell down before his face; and they said, Behold, we be thy servants.

THE END OF JOSEPH

And Joseph said unto them, Fear not; for am I in the place of God? And as for you, ye meant evil against me; but God meant it for good, to bring to pass, as it is this day, to save much people alive. Now therefore fear ye not; I will nourish you, and your little ones. And he comforted them, and spake kindly unto them.

[And Joseph dwelt in Egypt, he, and his father's house; and Joseph lived an hundred and ten years.]

And Joseph saw Ephraim's children of the third generation; the children also of Machir the son of Manasseh were born upon Joseph's knees. And Joseph said unto his brethren, I die; but God will surely visit you, and bring you up out of this land unto the land which he sware to Abraham, to Isaac, and to Jacob. And Joseph took an oath of the children of Israel, saying, God will surely visit you, and ye shall carry up my bones from hence. So Joseph died, being an hundred and ten years old; and they embalmed him, and he was put in a coffin in Egypt.

THE UNKNOWN HOMER OF THE HEBREWS

THE UNKNOWN HOMER OF THE HEBREWS[1]

THE Hellenic Homer was separated from the era of authentic Greek history and literature by a space of centuries almost blank to modern scholars. Dispute about his time and place, his personality and work, began as early as Herodotus, and has never ended. Whether he wrote or recited, and whether the oldest literary dialect of the Greeks had graphic form in his day, are not wholly settled questions. It has been disputed whether the work to which his name was attached was wholly or mainly his. The two great epics have been resolved by some into a series of dactylic tales and ballads, chanted and developed by more than one minstrel, and finally wrought into a continuous web of pictured lays.

But Homer came down to historic time in Greece as a name, and it stood for the genius who in unrecorded days sang deeds of heroes, and wove in immortal verse the "tale of Troy divine," and the adventurous wanderings of the returning

[1] Reprinted from *The New World*, March, 1897.

Odysseus. It came to stand for an imposing personality, more revered for the mystery out of which it came, more distinct to the imagination because of the little knowledge men had of its reality.

Almost contemporaneous with Homer, the epic genius of the Hebrews wrought in silence and obscurity, but in the midst of a stirring time in the experience of that ancient people, and after the opening of a literary period which closed only with their history. It was an age of records more continuous and complete, more authentic and better preserved, than any other of equal antiquity; and yet, if the name of the writer who contributed the grandest part to the Epic of Israel ever emerged into the light, it was soon lost. His work was broken in pieces and wrought with other material into a composite fabric of perdurable strength, and his personality was effaced. For twenty-five centuries and more, the Homer of the Hebrews has been without name and without personal identity.

It is one of the triumphs of modern Biblical research to have rescued the Hebrew genius from the oblivion in which it was buried by ages of superstition and imperfect knowledge. For a long time the ancient incrustations and the later deposits of bones and dust were guarded by the fierce glare of religous faith; but of late the protecting blaze has subsided, and, in the sober light of knowledge and reason, excavations have been made which reveal the true character of the hidden treasure. In this the work of the Hebrew Homer is easily traced by its golden quality, broken and mixed as it is with baser metal.

In that sacred history of the ancient Hebrews into whose texture the "laws" of Judaism were woven after the restoration of the temple by the returned captives of Babylon, critics have been able to distinguish with clearness certain superior material which has come to be known as the "Jehovist document." Curtailed as it had been, and somewhat mingled with other substance, it is for the most part separable from the rest. It was in the process of later combination that this precious document became broken and deranged, and imbedded in a conglomerate mass.

Study of the Hellenic Homer's work in relation to events and authorship is much more a matter of conjecture now than study of the writings of the Hebrew Homer, whose early obscurity and later oblivion were due to circumstances peculiar to the character and history of Israel. The people of Ephraim had drifted from an exclusive devotion to Jehovah from the time that Jeroboam set up his symbols of worship at Bethel and Dan. The Phœnician princess, whom Ahab made his queen, established the luxurious cult of Baal and Astarte above the humbler forms of worship of the God of Israel, and pursued the prophets with cruel persecutions, driving those who escaped slaughter to the mountains and caves. But after Jehu had accomplished his bloody revolution, and dogs had eaten the flesh of Jezebel in the streets of Jezreel, there was a revival of the ancient faith and the teachers of Israel began their great work.

It was not far from this time that the epic genius appeared who wove from shreds of Chaldean fable and Phœnician myth the marvellous tale of the early world, and out of ancestral traditions that had sprung from familiar names and places wrought the story of the covenant with Abraham, the inheritance of Jacob, and the great deliverance from the bondage of Egypt, which put the people of Israel under such tremendous obligation of submission and fidelity to Jehovah their God. To impress them with this, and to secure their obedience to commands necessary to hold them to their allegiance, was doubtless the main purpose of this writer, but he displayed a creative genius in dealing with his material which has never been excelled in power.

While the parts of the ancient record into which the work of the great Jehovist was wrought are easily distinguished from the rest, we cannot tell how far he made use of material already existing in written or unwritten form, any more than we can tell how far Homer derived the episodes of the Iliad and the Odyssey from the floating tales and traditions of the time, and how far they were creations of his own brain. But there is no doubt that he gave a certain unity to what was before detached and incoherent, and transmuted his material with the fiery touch of genius that gave it durability and an unfading lustre. It is to the Jehovist writer that we owe the never-to-be-forgotten pictures of the Books of Genesis and Exodus.

Oppressed with what seemed to be a hopeless tendency to evil in mankind in his own day, but inspired by an invincible faith in the righteousness of Israel's God, and by a yearning for the purity and simplicity of the days when Israel's forefathers dwelt in tents, the Jehovist gave us the immortal story of the Garden of Eden and the fall of man, in which there was a strain of profound philosophy that has pervaded religious doctrine ever since. His sombre theory of human depravity was carried still further in the story of Cain and Abel, which showed that the innocent offspring of the first couple was slain, and only the guilty propagated the early generations of men, evolving but a single family worthy of preservation, when a disappointed deity destroyed the rest with a great flood. Little of the story of the Deluge, as it has come down to us, is from the pen of the Jehovist, but it was he who explained the event as the result of the repentance and grief of the Lord that he had made man, because "every imagination of the thoughts of his heart was only evil continually." He gave the touches most vividly remembered of the dismal rain of forty days and forty nights, the resting of the ark on Mount Ararat, and the sending forth of the raven and the dove; and he gave the hopeless turn to the covenant of the Lord, in return for sacrifice, that he would curse the ground no more for man's sake, "for that the imagination of his heart is evil from his youth." Touches of the same gloomy philosophy appear in the dispersion of the presumptuous tower-builders of Shinar.

It is in the Jehovist document that we can trace a continuous line of ethnic myths with wonderful depth and variety of meaning. The writer had at his command, in oral or written form, stories of the patriarchs, or imagined ancestors of the people; some of them perhaps existed in more than one version, but it was in the use made of them that the power of his genius mainly appears. The common progenitor of the Semitic peoples was consecrated as the special ancestor of Israel by a covenant with the Lord (Jehovah); and it is the Jehovist who gives us the impressive picture of the wanderer from Ur of the Chaldees beneath the numberless stars, when a deep sleep and a horror of great darkness fell upon him, as the solemn prophecy of affliction and deliverance was made, and the weird vision of a smoking furnace and a flaming torch passed over the sacrifice of the covenant.

The line of the ethnic myths of Israel is clearly traceable in the writings of the Jehovist, from Ararat to Sinai. The curse of Canaan for the gross filial disrespect of one of the sons of Noah was enough to justify and explain the contempt and menial servitude in which the tribes were held that Israel had subjugated. Early death was a sign of divine disfavor, and before Abram set out to take possession of the land which was to be the heritage of his posterity, the brother died who was to be the ancestor of Israel's traditional enemies, Moab and Ammon; and though his son Lot, through Abram's intervention, was saved from the fate of Sodom, it was in hideous incest that the hated Moabites and Ammonites had their origin.

The people of the Arabian deserts were thrust out from the family of Abraham in the quaint story of Ishmael and his Egyptian mother, while Israel's origin was sanctified by divine promise in the only son of the "princess" (Sarah), whose very name (Isaac) was expressive of joy. In the charming tale of the marriage of Isaac with Rebekah is figured the ancient amity with Syria, and in it also the later alliance of that country with Northern Israel is sanctified. Most deeply expressive of all mythic stories is that of the twin children of the Syrian mother, the warlike hunters of the red and shaggy region of Edom and Mount Seir, and the peaceful dwellers in tents who supplanted these by superiority of mental resource and the potency of paternal blessing.

In the lonely journey of Jacob to the land of his mother's nativity, and the vision of renewed promise on the ancient height of Luz, there is a strain of exalted poetry. As Jacob embodied with marvellous condensation the characteristics of Israel as a race, so in the birth of his sons by the two Syrian wives and their handmaids was figured with a few clear strokes the origin and relationship of the tribes. Again, the superior skill of Israel and the success that comes from divine favor were illustrated in the acquisition of Laban's property, and out of the jealousy and quarrels which it engendered came the ancient division of possessions and the establishment of the bounds of Syria.

The story of Joseph, which has charmed so many generations of the children of men, both young and old, is at once an exaltation of the people of the Northern Kingdom of Israel and a mythical explanation of the falling of the tribes under the sway of Egypt, and their preservation there until deliverance came. The form in which we have it is a blending of two different versions, but it is in the epic material of the Jehovist that we find those episodes and expressions that always live in the memory. It is he who tells us of the father's peculiar affection, and of its token in the long-sleeved tunic (the "coat of many colors"), and of the triumphant test of virtue in the house of the Egyptian master. The experience in prison, and the liberation through the interpretation of dreams, are from another hand, as, for the most part, is the account of the exaltation to power and the first visit of the famine-stricken brethren. But all the touching passages with reference to the sad old patriarch in the land of Canaan, and his tender fondness for the remaining child of his old age; the yearning of Pharaoh's officer, amid his grandeur, toward the humble visitors from his father's house, and especially for the one brother who was his own mother's son; Judah's pathetic plea, and Joseph's weeping revelation of himself, — in short, all those strokes that touch the everlasting fountains of human joy and sorrow, — came from the Homeric teller of Israel's ancient story.

But not alone the covenant and promise that bound a heedless and faithless people to submission to their mighty deity was the theme of that ancient and unknown genius of the Hebrew race. He had to tell of the still more sacred bond of gratitude that came from the fulfilment of promise in the deliverance from Egyptian bondage, the passage of a drear and hostile wilderness, and full possession of the land which the people now enjoyed. Centuries had gone by, and traditions of those wonderful experiences, which had long passed from generation to generation by word of mouth, had grown dim. The conflicts of the kingdoms, the lapses from the worship of Jehovah, the making of written records, and the diversion of men's minds from the treasured past, were making the people forgetful of their sacred heritage and their obligations to the national God.

No doubt the traditions of deliverance from Egyptian bondage gathered around the name of Moses, who had held the escaping people to obedience and discipline through fear of the terrible deity in whose name he spoke; but it was the Jehovist writer who created the august figure of the deliverer and the lawgiver which has overshadowed Judaism to this day. Not all of the story of the Exodus is from his pen, but to him we owe the picture of Moses as a herdsman in Midian when the God of his people revealed himself in fire in the wilderness of Mount Horeb and gave the promise of deliverance. It was he who first told of the signs and wonders wherewith Pharaoh was constrained to let the people go, — of the guidance by flame and smoke; the passage of the Red Sea; and the awful theophany of Mount Sinai, when the trumpet blew so loud. All this led up to the first divine commands whose ineffaceable durability was symbolized by the writing of God's finger on tables of stone.

The grandiose conceptions of this writer, and the power with which he gave them expression, make him the veritable Homer of the Hebrews, albeit his purpose was so much more than his personality that men failed to record his name. Personality and authorship were deemed of no account when his work was used as raw material and mingled with other matter by a prosaic compiler. The work, broken and disfigured though it be, can be identified, but the author remains in mystery.

The composition of the work perhaps began in those troublous days of Ahab and Jezebel, when the prophets were slain or driven to concealment in the caves of the mountains. There is suggested a coincidence in ancient Hebrew history that fascinates the imagination. The episodes of Elijah and Elisha, incorporated in the Book of Kings, with their miracles and marvels, were mostly taken from the *haggadas* of a time much later than the events with which they are connected. But they give us the picture of one of those potent prophets who always appeared as watchmen of the Lord in Israel in critical times. He may have lurked here and there on the borders of Syria or Phœnicia, getting word of the wicked ways of Ahab, who sought his death as a "troubler of Israel." He may have sojourned in obscure abodes and concealed himself from time to time on Mount Carmel. In moods of desperation he may have retired to the solitudes of Mount Horeb and found new inspiration in the "still, small voice" of God in the desert wildernesses. Watching for his hour and covering his movements with mystery, he may have had a decisive hand in the revolutions at Damascus and Samaria when Hazael and Jehu usurped the thrones of Benhadad and Ahab, and made way for the revival of Jehovah's power in the land of Ephraim.

If this be so, may not one of the productions of the great religious ferment, which then began, have been the sacred history of Israel which embodied the covenant with Abraham, the promise to Jacob, the preservation by Joseph, the deliverance through Moses, and set forth the commands of the great Jehovah? May not the author of this production have been the mysterious prophet of Mount Carmel who was the terror of Jezebel and the hope of Israel in a dark and bloody time, and whose personality was veiled behind the names of Elijah and Elisha?

HISTORY, PROPHECY, AND THE MONUMENTS.

BY

JAMES F. McCURDY, PH.D., LL.D.

Volumes I. and II. Each $3.00, *net*. Volume III. *In Preparation.*

"Professor McCurdy's work is one of which American scholarship has reason to feel proud. . . . The announcement that only a few months after its appearance a second edition of the first volume has been called for is a testimony alike to the satisfactory character of the work and to the need that existed for just such a presentation as Professor McCurdy has furnished. He takes up in succession the northern Semites, Babylonians, Canaanites, Egyptians, Hittites, Aramæans, and Assyrians, and treats of their relations, political and religious, to the Hebrews, from the earliest time down to the destruction of the northern Hebrew kingdom in 722 B.C. In the second volume the subject will be continued through the Persian period of supremacy in Western Asia. We look forward with interest to the continuation of Professor McCurdy's work. It is to be heartily recommended to the general public as a very useful compendium. For Bible readers and Bible students alike, it is an invaluable guide." — PROF. MORRIS JASTROW, Jr., in the *New World.*

SOCIAL EVOLUTION.

BY

BENJAMIN KIDD.

NEW EDITION, REVISED, WITH A NEW PREFACE.

Crown 8vo. Cloth. Price $1.50.

"It is a study of the whole development of humanity in a new light, and it is sustained and strong and fresh throughout. . . . It is a profound work, which invites the attention of our ablest minds, and which will reward those who give it their careful and best thought. It marks out new lines of study, and is written in that calm and resolute tone which secures the confidence of the reader. It is undoubtedly the ablest book on social development that has been published for a long time." — *Boston Herald.*

"Those who wish to follow the Bishop of Durham's advice to his clergy — 'to think over the questions of socialism, to discuss them with one another reverently and patiently, but not to improvise hasty judgments' — will find a most admirable introduction in Mr. Kidd's book on social evolution. It is this, because it not merely contains a comprehensive view of the very wide field of human progress, but is packed with suggestive thoughts for interpreting it aright. . . . We hope that the same clear and well-balanced judgment that has given us this helpful essay will not stay here, but give us further guidance as to the principles which ought to govern right thinking on this the question of the day. We heartily commend this really valuable study to every student of the perplexing problems of socialism." — *The Churchman.*

THE MACMILLAN COMPANY,
66 FIFTH AVENUE, NEW YORK.

Small 18mo. Cloth extra, 50 cents each; Leather, 60 cents.

The Modern Reader's Bible.

A Series of Books from the Sacred Scriptures, presented in Modern Literary Form.

BY

RICHARD G. MOULTON,

M.A. (Camb.), Ph.D. (Penn.),

Professor of Literature in English in the University of Chicago.

By permission we quote the following

COMMENTS.

"'The Modern Reader's Bible' is altogether admirable and of special value."
HENRY C. POTTER,
Bishop of the Protestant Epis. Church.

"To the student, and to all persons who relish truth in its finest form of expression, it is a positive boon."
JOHN F. HURST,
Bishop of the Methodist Epis. Church.

"The low price of the little volumes puts them within the reach of the great majority of American households, and I look for a large increase of interest in the Bible, for a much better understanding of its general spirit and teaching, and especially for an increased appreciation of its inspirational power, from the publication of the Modern Reader's Bible."
LYMAN ABBOTT,
Editor-in-Chief of The Outlook.

"Professor Moulton has inaugurated a new epoch in Bible study, and it is not too much to pronounce it one of the most important spiritual and literary events of the times. . . . Each volume contains a very valuable introductory study of the book presented as a piece of literature. . . . The text is that of the Revised Version." — *Biblia.*

"We have so often expressed our high opinion of the scholarly qualities exhibited in this series, as well as of the publishers' success in putting it before the public, that we hardly need add anything now. The editor's intent to bring out distinguishingly the literary value of the Bible is most successfully accomplished." — *Congregationalist*, Boston.

"No literary enterprise of our day promises larger results than the Modern Reader's Bible. . . . In this series of works the Sacred Scriptures are presented in modern literary form by one of the ablest living English scholars, Professor Moulton. No university professor in English, in our time, has awakened more widespread interest in the study of English classical literature than he. On questions of literary interest there is no higher authority, and no more competent man could be found for this work of quickening literary interest in the Bible." *The Mail and Empire*, Toronto.

THE MACMILLAN COMPANY,
66 FIFTH AVENUE, NEW YORK.

www.ingramcontent.com/pod-product-compliance
Lightning Source LLC
Chambersburg PA
CBHW020225240426
43672CB00006B/422